THE HOME RECORDING HANDBOOK

Martin Newell

DUNLIN PRESS

THE HOME RECORDING HANDBOOK
Martin Newell
Published by Dunlin Press in 2025

Dunlin Press
Wivenhoe, Essex
dunlinpress.com | @dunlinpress

The right of Martin Newell to be identified as the author of this work has been asserted in accordance with Section 77 of the Copyright, Designs and Patents Act 1988.

This book is sold subject to the condition that it shall not, by way of trade of otherwise, be lent, resold, hired out or otherwise circulated without the publisher's prior consent in any form of binding or cover other than which it is published and without a similar condition including this condition being imposed on the subsequent purchaser. No part of this publication may be reproduced, stored in or introduced into a retrieval system, or transmitted, in any form, or by any means (electronic, mechanical, photocopying, recording or otherwise) without the prior written permission of the publisher. Any person who does any unauthorised act in relation to this publication may be liable to criminal prosecution and civil claims for damages.

A CIP record of this book is available from the British Library.

ISBN: 978-1-7394038-5-0

Set in Futura and Avant Garde Gothic Pro
Book illustration and design by Ella Johnston.

To David Hoser – from whom I learned much.

Aged 13, in my gran's kitchen.

"I was a teenage twat."

D.I.Y

- Why Can't I Hear Anything? — 6
- My First Tape Recorder — 12
- Yamaha Dynamic Guitar 1965 — 18
- The Sony Grail — 22
- How England Got its Echo — 28
- Back to Home Recording — 34
- Bloody Boring Waffle About Speakers and Cans — 42
- My Guitars — 48
- Only the Shadows Know — 54
- On the Bus with Cliff — 58
- Residential Pampering — 64
- Drumfoolery: A Personal History of Drums and Percussion — 70
- How I Wrote a New National Anthem — 78
- My Old Piano — 84
- In Berlin with Christo — 90
- Giving Voice — 96
- Why DIY? — 102
- Songwriting for Dummies — 108
- They Read the Flyshit: Re-examining Classical Music — 114
- The Rolling Stones in Hyde Park — 120
- Meanwhile… in Abbey Road — 126
- How We Forgot to Write Songs — 132
- Don't… Take it Easy — 136
- The Sixties — 142
- Pop Festivals 50 Years On — 146
- In Andy's Shed — 150
- Rock Stars' Other Talents — 156
- Space — 162

WHY CAN'T I HEAR ANYTHING?

A friend and longtime former bandmate of mine, Ian Peppercorn, used to have a printed sign just above the recording desk in his home studio. The sign read 'Why Can't I Hear Anything?' That plaintive phrase sums up pretty much all of the feelings of frustration, despair and bewilderment commonly experienced when the creative musician comes up against the mysterious shortcomings of their technology.

I mean, there you are at last, in your own little den, with all your equipment and instruments primed and ready to go. The recorder is switched on and all its little lights are blinking optimistically. Perhaps you've invited someone round to listen to some recent work? Maybe you've got a guitar or a microphone standing by, ready to put that immortal performance onto your latest masterpiece.

You press 'play'. There's nothing. You plug some headphones in, listening intently. Nothing. You remove the headphones and listen. There's still nothing. You check the speakers. They're on. Nothing. You study the meters of the track you've just recorded. You can see a signal. So you've now confirmed, at least, that you have a recording. You check again. Maybe a faulty headphone jack? You plug another set of headphones in. There's still nothing. You take the headphones off. You crane your head over the top of the desk. You crawl around underneath the desk. Nothing. Through clenched teeth, and with a deep sigh, you ask, "Why can't I fucking hear anything?"

The answer to the question above is often, "It's probably a cable." But not always. Sometimes the answer is, "You've probably forgotten to switch something on – or off." But not always. Carry on, then.

Sometimes while recording, just prior to doing a take, you'll sometimes hear a buzz. Or an annoying hum. For years I used a homemade bass built by Carl Szymanski, the bassist in my first proper band Plod. It was great. But sometimes it emitted just such a hum. This was possibly caused by some minor earth loop. Its intermittency was the vexing thing. It wasn't always there. My cure for it was to get a wire, attach one end to one of the strings below the bridge, then put the other end down my sock so that I became the earthing for it, while still being able to use both of my hands to play the guitar.

One aspect of home-recording, for me, is that I've often been able to fix problems – without being able to show my workings. I kept my Sony TC630 going for the last two years of its life by jamming a Hawaiian steel guitar roller up against a tape-guide. This kept the transport stable so that the tape travelled safely past the heads, capstan and pinch-roller. Unconventional? Yes. Wrong? Possibly. Did it work? Yep.

In the early days of the Cleaners from Venus, we had no microphone stands. We were that poor. When Lol Elliott and I first started recording together, we miked up his kit in the following manner. For the bass drum, we took one cheap microphone, wrapped it in a cushion with its head sticking out. We then positioned the mic inside the bass drum, using a house-brick on top of the cushion in order to hold it in place. Next, we took a broomstick and stuck it through the elliptical seat aperture of an old science lab stool. Now we Sellotaped another cheap microphone to the top of the broomstick. We positioned this mic somewhere between the hi-hat and the snare drum, leaning it until we got it at the required angle. Now we dug out a third microphone. We sellotaped this one onto an overhead light fitting, hanging it about 20 inches above the drums. We plugged all three microphones into the WEM Copicat inputs, setting the unit to a mild slapback echo. Finally, I plugged the homemade bass into the fourth Copicat input. Now I took a jack lead out of the Copicat and fed the whole shebang into my tape recorder. For about a year, every Monday, that was how the Cleaners from Venus recorded bass and drums for *Blow Away Your Troubles*, our first cassette album.

This, of course, was before I'd managed to save up enough to buy my first Tascam Portastudio 144. Over four decades later, some of the songs on that first cassette have become world-famous multi-million streaming lo-fi classics. People have even tried to replicate our sound. I had a letter just the other day, in fact, asking how we got that fantastic bass sound? No idea. Eat your heart out, Abbey Road.

By my mid-20s, I'd realised that if I was to carry on producing music in the way I wanted to do it, then I'd have to do so without the music business and its media. A small thing standing in my way was that I hardly had any money and nearly nobody had ever heard of me. I was working as a kitchen porter four days a week. There was sometimes an extra night's shift I could take, which meant I could save towards a new recorder. It was slow going. At this time I just about earned enough to pay my rent and to buy luxuries like food. As for necessities like beer, I learned how to make my own and I became rather good at it. But I was still struggling to become the kind of recording artist that I was hoping to be. I was now used to being rejected, of course. I was also used to the sound of small-town laughter whenever I told anyone what I was trying to do. Upon hearing the Cleaners from Venus's early work – which often featured songs about aliens, unsuitable romances and nuclear war – people thought we were peculiar, if not actually damaged. But I also knew how to write good songs. That could not be taken away from me.

I still love home recording. I suppose that in all these years I must have become better at it. But I still necessarily regard myself as an inspired amateur, rather than a trained professional. In some ways, with home recording, I've built myself a cage to be brilliant in. This is possibly how I've managed to prevent my creativity from being stifled by what some call the 'tyranny of choice' a temptation presented to us nowadays by a vast ocean of new technological advances.

    Inside me, somewhere, however, remains that 12-year-old boy, experimenting with his first tape recorder: making it play at different speeds, and finding out what a dog bark sounds like played backwards. In those days there were many happy and hilarious accidents. The possibilities seemed endless. In some ways, they still do. I don't want it to ever become too efficient, too organised, too 'professional'. Such things aren't always what pop music and the recording of it are really about. One more time then. "Why can't I hear anything?" It's a question I'm still asking myself. Welcome to home recording. Don't forget to have fun.

MY FIRST TAPE RECORDER

It is useful to know how to record those sounds that don't, strictly-speaking, qualify as music. Not everything I've recorded has been connected with making music.

Come with me now to Singapore, somewhere in the summer of 1965. One day, a tape recorder arrived at our home. It had come out of my dad's office. A small portable device, probably a Philips, with little three-inch tape-reels, it had previously been used for dictation. With the arrival of a superior dictation recorder, my considerate father thought that it might be the sort of thing I would be interested in.

Too damned right I was interested. Although I hadn't yet got my first guitar, at 12 years old I already knew that this tape recorder was somehow tied up with my destiny. It had a rubbishy little microphone and a handful of pre-loved tape reels. It was, however, enough. I immediately began jotting down ideas for plays, spoof adverts and comedy sketches. I began recording everything I could: the dog barking; people outside in the street; my mum speaking to her friends; and pop songs I'd heard on the radio. What a pain I must have been.

Next, I learned that by changing the tape recorder's speeds, I could slow down or speed up voices with (to me) hilarious results. I learned that by flipping one of the little tape-reels over and carefully twisting the tape once, I could make pre-recorded sounds come out backwards.

I found this stuff enthralling. I had a good mate, Graham, who lived in the flat-block opposite me. He also had a tape recorder. Together, during the school holidays, we devised a play about time travel. At one point we needed the noise of an excited crowd. So, the two of us started making the appropriate noises. Then we played the first recording of the 'crowd' on my tape recorder's tiny speaker. We played this first recording as loud as it would go while we simultaneously recorded ourselves on Graham's tape recorder making more 'crowd' noises. Three more turns repeating this procedure resulted in quite a convincing (to us) crowd effect. It was muffled, it was hissy, but we'd done something very important, something groundbreaking, in fact. We'd created a rudimentary kind of over-dubbing.

Unfortunately, we didn't yet know about fading tracks in or out. Nor did we know what sound-mixing entailed. But, for two lads messing around with tape recorders it remained a breakthrough of sorts. I now regard this event as being akin to the moment in the film *2001: A Space Odyssey* where the ape throws the bone spinning in slow motion up into the air, having made the world's first weapon. Graham and I would only have needed the Richard Strauss soundtrack in the background and we'd have been set.

About a year later, upon returning to England, and having acquired my first guitar, for the next few months I continued to record the pop charts from the radio every week so that I could try to teach myself any songs I liked. I rarely recorded either my own singing or guitar playing. Nor did I persist in recording my early songwriting efforts. All of these items, recorded within the confines of a teenage bedroom, sounded ego-demolishingly terrible. It would only be after recording a song in my parents' empty garage that I realised what was missing from my home-recorded sound. One word. Reverb.

What I did soon find, however, was that I and another schoolmate, Dave Ward could write and record quite funny comedy sketches. Predictably, they were crude, primitive and sometimes plain wrong. But we did find them endlessly amusing. At least it kept us off the streets.

Decades later, I now realise that my hours making those tapes taught me a hell of a lot. I grew up, or rather, *failed* to grow up, in the 1960s. It was a time in which comedy and novelty records were popular. So popular were they in those days that they often made the charts. Benny Hill, Charlie Drake, the pre-disgraced Rolf Harris, the Goons, Anthony Newley, Morecambe and Wise and many other artistes made such discs. Comedy records still possessed a legitimacy back then, something which has long-since evaporated. Nearly nobody nowadays, in the pompous and self-reverential world of modern pop, wants to compromise their fragile artistic dignity by making people laugh.

It's worth mentioning that Sir George Martin, the Beatles producer, prior to working with the band, had chiefly been a producer of comedy records for the Parlophone label, a name that soon became synonymous with Fab Four themselves. I can't be the first to conclude that George Martin's versatility and ingenuity as a producer was almost certainly honed by his time working in the demanding arena of comedy records. Working with people like the Goons and Bernard Cribbins would have surely have prepped him well for the needs of the Beatles during their psychedelic period.

Sound effects, were also something in which I took a huge interest, right from my days with that first tape recorder. I had to teach myself what every sound-effects person and film 'foley' artist eventually learns.

I call this lesson 'A Pub is Not a Pub'. If, during the course of recording, you should ever need the authentic sound of a British pub – don't go to a pub. You won't find the sound there. What you'll find instead, is all manner of stuff that you don't want on your recording: the low hum of beer coolers; an electronic till; creaking doors and shouted orders from a nearby kitchen. There may be the sounds of buses and lorries passing the building. In fact, you'll probably get everything but the warm hubbub of voices, punctuated by occasional laughter, that you'd originally aimed to record.

So, how do you get a pub atmosphere such as the one you might hear on an afternoon radio play? Well, the easiest way is to buy a CD of BBC Sound Effects. Or you could possibly lift some free ones from the internet.

I actually bought a small 1950s library of sound effects on Ebay for $7. It had loads of old Warner Bros/Hanna Barbera-style cartoon sounds. I also concocted my own pub-sound foley too, by over-dubbing bits of conversation and laughter until I had a suitably authentic mix. My own go-to pub background, however, is actually a recording of a quiet Czech bar, which some uncredited recordist made. There's no music or clinking of glasses, only the sound of about a dozen people, talking softly. You honestly can't hear that the voices aren't speaking in English. But the recording possesses exactly the close-up cosy warmth which I associate with an English country boozer on a medium-busy evening.

It can be fun and challenging making sound effects. If, for instance I want the effect of someone making a quick getaway, there's a classic cartoon method of doing so. It's a rapid three-second burst on bongo drums combined with a bullet ricochet effect sliced in at the end. It makes a 'Budda-budda-budda-budda-peeyow!' sound. Absolutely nothing like the sound of someone running away, but for comic effect it conveys the impression well.

One last thing about sound effects: it's not necessarily just an occupation for stupid boys who never grow up. Sound Effects Assistant once used to be a legitimate job in BBC Radio. No less a luminary than Dame Esther Rantzen began her career in this post. I actually remember watching a TV clip of her giving a small demonstration of the art. So remember, in sound effects a pub is not (necessarily) a pub.

LESSON 1
NOT EVERYONE WILL BE INTERESTED IN YOUR MUSIC

Not everyone will always understand your need to get the world down on tape. Two friends of mine decided to go out one day into the Essex countryside to record 'an album' of some of their songs, live with a natural sonic backdrop. In the middle of their proceedings, the farmer whose land it was came over and shouted at them, "Whatever d'you think you're doing?" Or words to that effect. He then went on shouting at them while they made their apologies and packed up their stuff. The result was a cassette album entitled *Interrupted by Farmer* by the Orphans of Babylon – Giles Smith and Geoff Lawrence – recordings of short and funny songs, usually less than two minutes long. Very listenable they were too. For more sensitive artistes making their first forays into recording, I'd say, do go out and get the world down on tape. But don't expect it to play ball with you, because very often, it won't.

YAMAHA DYNAMIC GUITAR 1965

It arrived for Christmas 1965. I was 12 years old. My family had been living in Singapore for about 16 months. I'd asked, hoping against hope, for a drum-kit. I got a guitar, a six-string Yamaha acoustic. It arrived at Nee Soon Garrison via a Chinese trader who drove around the camp in a van. He could usually get you pretty much anything that the NAAFI (Navy, Army and Air Force Institutes) shop didn't sell. The guitar would change my life, dictating directly or indirectly much of everything I've experienced since.

At first I could only play it one string at a time, using a thumb and one finger. Back at school in January 1966, it was announced that for any pupils who'd recently acquired guitars, there would be elementary lessons available as an extra-curricular activity. A young science teacher, recently arrived from England – a folk musician as it happened – had volunteered to teach half a dozen of us a few guitar basics. The first thing we learned was how to tune our guitars, from either one note on a piano or, if we had one, a set of pitch pipes.

Next, we learned that a chord was a combination of notes which, when strummed together with other chords, could be used to accompany, say, the singing of a song. We learned our first tune, 'Bobby Shaftoe', using a basic claw-hammer plucking method, repeated over two alternating chords. For those pre-teenage pop stars among us who'd been hoping to rattle off 'A Hard Day's Night', this was something of a disappointment.

Some of us had already glimpsed pop stardom only just around the corner. It wouldn't matter anymore that we couldn't play football or have a fight. Who cared that we were useless at maths? Or that we were spotty little nobodies that no girl would even glance at? In our own fevered minds, we were already potentially the next Beatles or Stones. As soon as we'd mastered a few songs, we'd be in the charts. By then, the second that we dared to venture out of our front doors, screaming fans would pursue us. We'd soon be earning enough money not to have to do as our parents told us, ever again.

There used to be small ad in the back of certain boyhood publications. It depicted a lad with a quiff, holding a guitar up in jaunty Hank Marvin-style, while a group of delighted partygoers looked admiringly on. The small ad said, 'Learn to Play the Guitar in Three Weeks. Be popular at parties, entertain people and make new friends.' Well, 'Bobby Shaftoe' seemed a long way from that possibility. Yet, in three simple lessons I'd already improved. Everything I've learned subsequently sprang from those first steps. Over the decades I've had a lot to thank that folkie science teacher for.

In mid-April 1966, having just turned 13, I returned to England after almost two years in Singapore. My father had been posted up-country to the jungle highlands of Malaya. It was a struggle to convince my parents to let me take my guitar on the flight home. But I did it. I'd be living with my grandparents for a least a yearand attending a secondary modern school in Harpenden, Hertfordshire.

England, in my absence, had gone from a monochrome place of rainy terraces and steam trains, to a go-go dancing, pirate-radio paradise. It was now in swinging Eastmancolor. In 1966, brilliant new pop singles came out every hour, on-the-hour. The songs embedded themselves in my heart in such a way that I've never forgotten them. I don't think I was alone. There was just something special about that era in pop music.

I still have the original Yamaha guitar that the man in the van had delivered in December 1965. I don't play it much these days but it hangs in my kitchen. In 1976 it was painted for me by a rather talented girlfriend. "What would you like me to paint on it?" she'd asked. I blithely replied, "Aw, I dunno, something like Gustav Klimt, maybe?" As if she'd just be able to knock off something like that. Three days later, she'd done it. After stripping the original varnish off, she had indeed just knocked off a Klimt impression. Not bad for a young woman fresh out of Essex Uni with an Art History degree.

The guitar itself? Well, I didn't know this when I was a beginner, but it had a terrible action. Learning bar chords on it was like playing an egg-slicer. The instrument went everywhere with me, all through my teens and beyond.

When I was broke and couldn't afford new strings, I'd take the old ones off and boil them up with a bit of vinegar in order to brighten their sound. The guitar was my constant companion and, from age 15, my main songwriting tool. Now, nearly six decades later, when at home, I'm still rarely more than a few yards away from it.

LESSON 2
LOOK AFTER YOUR STRINGS

Strings can be expensive and we can't always afford to keep loads of spares. But it's handy to have them, say, in the middle of a recording session, when you or another player suddenly needs to replace a broken string and the shops aren't open. When changing a set of strings, if the old set are really grungy, boil them up in an old saucepan for five minutes or so, adding about an eggcup of vinegar. Doing this will clean all the muck and the grease off the strings. Wind them up and store them in a packet. It won't make them brand new again, but it will brighten them up sufficiently for use as emergency replacements for one session. This method works especially well on bass guitar strings which will often go dull rather than actually break.

THE SONY GRAIL

Carl the bass-player and I picked it up from a hi-fi shop in Chelmsford. The 'Machine Which Changed My Life' arrived when I was 21 years old. A tiny insurance policy came to maturity, which my prudent mum had taken out for me shortly after I was born. In March 1974 it came to about £160. I knew exactly what I wanted. I'd seen one before. A student at the nearby University of Essex had used one to record the music for a theatre production I'd attended. The minute I saw it I knew that I needed this gizmo. The machine was a Sony TC630.

It was a reel-to-reel solid-state tape machine with three recording heads. It could operate at three different speeds. With it came two pretty impressive 15-watt speakers and a couple of half-decent microphones. The really amazing thing about it, however, was that it had an echo/reverb facility. It worked in stereo but if you wanted to multitrack, you could do so in mono. The TC630 was the nearest thing within its budget to a Tascam Portastudio, a piece of kit which would not come onto the market for almost another seven years.

First invented by Sony in 1969, the TC630 wasn't something which many people possessed. Rather too lo-fi for the rapidly expanding recording industry, conversely it was possibly too complex and expensive for beginners. For a 20-year-old Newell, however, it seemed a perfect songwriting tool, a demo machine and, at a push, the basis of a home recording studio.

At that age, apart from on TV documentaries, I'd never even seen a proper recording studio. The nearest it got – and this was rare – were one or two home-recording set-ups. They usually involved lots of eggboxes. Generally, some older, more tech-minded lad had acquired a Revox 4-track tape recorder, installing it in a spare bedroom, a garage or a shed. The first thing that everyone did to somehow affirm that this place was a 'professional' studio was to improvise some kind of soundproofing. There were three reasons for this process:

1) To keep the noise down so as not to disturb neighbours or family;
2) To provide insulation in order to stop neighbours and family noises disturbing the recordist;
3) To create a 'neutral' or dead sound in the recording room.

Eggboxes, so the legend went, absorbed the sound, creating a cheap version of a 'professional' studio acoustic.

Did it work? In my own experience? No. You just ended up with loads of eggboxes, usually glued to walls or hardboard screens. Often there were piles of those grey papier-mâché egg-trays hanging around, still unused after being collected and then abandoned in some corner. They looked horrible and as soon as you saw them, you knew that you weren't dealing with anything professional. Decades of home recording has taught me to just use the room I've got.

"It'll probably be okay," I usually say.

In any case, the early 1970s was possibly the worst time to aspire to the prevailing 'professional' studio acoustic, which usually sounded as if you'd been recording in a particularly full airing cupboard. The mission back then seemed to be to eliminate any trace of echo and reverb. "Going for honesty," was what I heard one hippy twat call it. One of its hallmarks was a snare-drum sound that approximated the dull thud of someone slapping their own knob on a cardboard shoebox.

Back in the mid-1970s, actual recording studios in the average small town tended to be 4-track affairs, with a limited range of sound processors and effects – 'toys' as we used to call them. Young bands, quite naturally, wanted to sound like their heroes. Upon discovering that they didn't, the singers always wanted more echo and reverb. The often older studio owner-engineers would usually caution them, "You don't wanna go swamping everything in echo and reverb." There was often a clash between inexperienced, insecure or egotistical young musicians and exasperated or tired studio engineers. Then, too, of course, the meter was always running, racking up the bill, a thing that added to the tension still further.

Good professional studios, even small ones, were generally beyond the budget of the average hometown hero. That's why you needed a record company to provide the money. So, you went into a small local studio with what you could afford, emerging after some hours with your demo. Usually, you'd be tired, disoriented and, sometimes, not quite satisfied with what you'd got. Then you went down to That London and 'did the rounds' of the record companies. This was if you'd been lucky enough to get an appointment. Then there was a wait for a phone call. Then you'd phone back a few times. There was rarely an answer. Then nothing happened.

Only very gradually did you learn that recording your music was in itself an art – one that was very different from playing live. It wasn't even remotely like all those documentaries and biopics that you'd seen. You didn't just swan into the place, smash out a couple of numbers, then have the engineer and producer do a high-five together, before shouting over the talk-back: "That was great, boys! You've just made your first Number One! Come up and have a listen."

You learned that recording your music was a long and irritating learning process. It's a cliché, but it's also true to say that the studio is in itself a separate instrument which advises that you learn to play it. That's why the Sony TC630 sound-on-sound recording machine, that I got just before my 21st birthday, was such a breakthrough for me.

Although it was laughably primitive by modern standards, before the invention of Tascam's 4-track portastudio the TC630 was the thing that taught me the most I'd learned so far about recording my own music. After I acquired it, I was able to double-track my vocals, play bass and guitar over a rhythm track and generally educate myself in basic studio-craft. Who cared if the results were only in hissy mono, or sometimes blighted by tape drop-outs? For me, it was the beginning of record production. The beginning of... well, everything, really.

LESSON 3
DOUBLE-UP YOUR VOCALS... SOMETIMES

In DIY music, natural double-tracking – that is, dubbing an identical vocal performance on top of one that you sang earlier – is a useful thing to know how to do when recording your vocals. It doesn't suit absolutely every song or even every type of music, but it can make an average pop-song vocal sparkle more, if it's done right.

To get one vocal performance smack-bang on top of an earlier vocal is not always the easiest thing to do. You might have to have take several runs at it or, if it's a bit tricky, take your time and do it one verse/chorus at a time. Speaking of which, you can choose to only double-track the vocals in the choruses, rather than cover the whole song. Doubling or even triple-tracking the choruses of a song will have the effect of emphasising them, thereby making them distinct from the verses. You don't have to get all the double-tracking exactly right, however. 'Close-enough' will sometimes do, as well as adding a certain charm. Another useful thing to do with double-tracking, is to leave the lesser of the two performances slightly quieter in volume than your best performance.

The immortal Sony TC 630 the machine that changed my life.

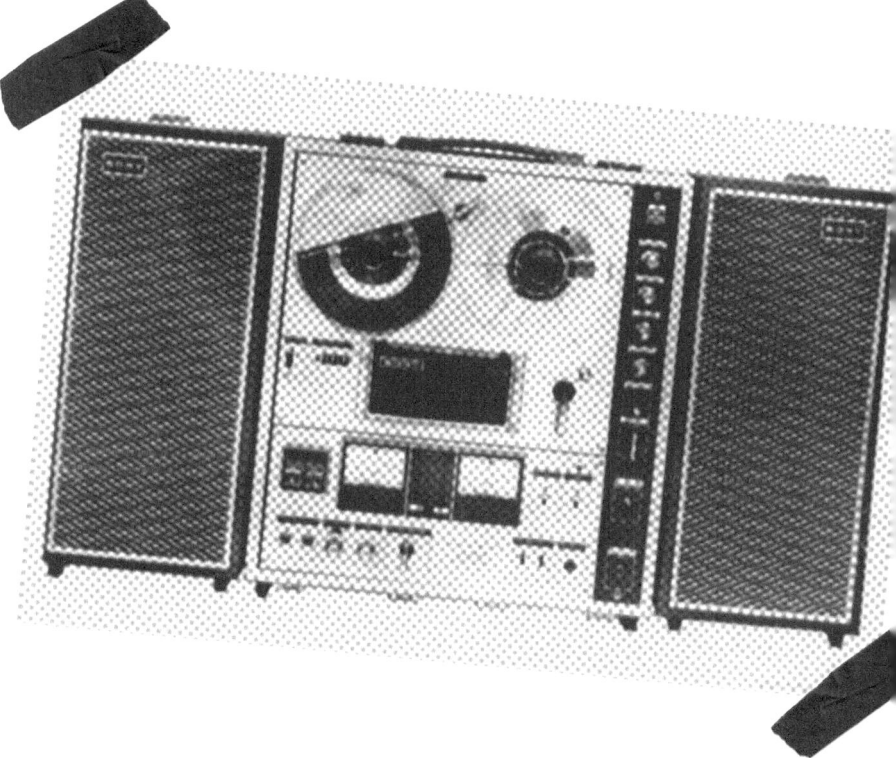

HOW ENGLAND GOT ITS ECHO

In autumn of 1967 my family relocated to Balham in south-west London. A pop-crazed 14-year-old with my first guitar, I went out one day in search of somewhere selling guitar strings. As I walked down Balham High Road I came to a guitar shop called Watkins Electric Music and wandered in, cautiously. A rather friendly bald bloke in his mid-40s emerged from somewhere at the back of the shop and asked, "What can I do you for?" I didn't realise it then but I'd just met Charlie Watkins, British audio engineer, legendary backroom boffin and the creator of the WEM Copicat, a now world-famous gizmo. Invented by Charlie with some help from a designer, he launched the echo unit in 1958 – just in time to give British rock'n'roll its distinctive echo.

Not wishing to bog you down in technology, the earliest Copicats were the size of a small toolbox, with the incongruously camp appearance of a 1950s vanity case. When you removed the lid and plugged it in, what you saw was a loop of recording tape rattling quietly over four tape-recorder heads. The tape's tension was regulated by a spring arm. The effect it gave was known as tape echo. Buttons on the appliance allowed guitarists to vary the effect from a short Elvis-style slapback or a stairwell-sized echo, right through to a full psychedelic freakout. What the Copicat actually did was to make even mediocre guitarists sound exotic and slightly dangerous. It was what my learned colleague Captain Sensible would probably describe as a 'talent booster'.

Charlie Watkins, a London Eastender born in 1923, joined the Merchant Navy aged 15 at the outset of WW2. Serving on the unarmed Atlantic convoys, as a young seaman he played an accordion in his spare time. More of his shipmates, however, played guitars. In an age before proper amplification, the young accordionist noted, guitarists often complained about the problems of being heard whenever they played with a band. After the war, Charlie, by now a record-shop owner, observed the rapidly growing popularity of the guitar. Recalling his shipmates' sound problems, he diversified into amplification, a subject which was still in its infancy in the 1950s. Thousands of British youngsters who'd taken up guitar during the short-lived skiffle boom now wanted to sound like their American rock 'n' roll heroes.

Charlie soon found himself with a small factory, making amplifiers and speakers. Thus was Watkins Electric Music born, or WEM as it soon became known. Decades after first wandering into his shop, I telephoned Charlie to ask him about the launch of the original Copicat. Typically modest, he remembered, "I only made ten at first. I wasn't sure how they were gonna do. But word must have got round. When I came to unlock the shop that Saturday morning there was a queue. At first I thought they must have been doing cut-price veg at the greengrocer's up the road. But they all wanted the Copicat. Johnny Kidd and the Pirates had the first one. Joe Brown bought one for Hank Marvin."

Over in their Chertsey factory, meanwhile, Charlie's two brothers Reg and Syd came up with the first mass-produced British electric guitar, the Watkins Rapier. With import duty on US guitars very high at that time, the Rapier's price made the possibility of becoming a rock star seem more do-able. It was the Copicat, however, that rockers of a certain age all remember. It gave early Brit-rock its distinctive shimmer, from 1958 right through the Sixties and beyond.

Near the turn of the Millennium when, after many requests, he manufactured a new version of the original analogue Copicat, Charlie told me that among the first people to make enquiries after it were Pink Floyd's Dave Gilmour and Dire Straits' Mark Knopfler. Very famous rock stars knew Charlie and often prevailed upon his knowledge. In the days before really big sound-rigs were common, the Rolling Stones, prior to their famous Hyde Park free concert, approached him to come up with a massive sound system; something bigger than anyone had used before. I was there. So was Charlie. You can see him in photos of the event, sitting up onstage, looking rather out of place among the rock aristocracy of the day.

As a young teenager, on rainy Saturdays I'd often go into Charlie's shop and just hang out. He never minded.

It was strange sometimes, hearing this ordinary, dad-like bloke talking so knowledgeably about the latest psychedelic bands. He once told me, "That Crazy World of Arthur Brown – they're gonna do alright. Just watch." Sure enough, three months later, The Crazy World of Arthur Brown had a massive Number One hit with 'Fire'. Displayed on the wall of his shop in the autumn of 1969, was a letter signed by all the Stones, thanking Charlie for the Hyde Park sound system. As I sometimes tell overseas music journalists, the people who made Britain great weren't always those Victorian blokes you see on statues, sitting on horses with feathered coal scuttles on their heads. Some of them wore brown cotton work-coats and carried soldering irons in their hands. Like Charlie Watkins.

LESSON 4
LEARN ABOUT ECHO, ECHO, ECHO...

Echo (sometimes known as 'delay') and reverb are an essential part of the home recordist's tool kit. For the not-so-technical among us reverb is the acoustic effect you'll hear in, say, a small hall, a large hall or a cathedral. Echo is what you'll hear when a particular sound bounces back, as if from a mountainside, as a repeat of itself or as a series of repeats. Charlie Watkins' Copicat echo unit was created in the 1950s using a loop of recording tape. Wonderful as it may have been for creating early rock'n'roll effects, modern delay and reverb units are infinitely more reliable, versatile and compact.

Many portable home-recording machines nowadays incorporate their own on-board reverb effects. Some of the Tascam Portastudio models, for instance, feature reverb settings which I think are really well-designed. Computer programmes such as Garageband and Audacity also provide a range of effects in drop-down menus. It's still worth, however, looking out for old guitar-pedal effects and the type of echo units that you can buy secondhand.

Echo can be quite hit and miss when you're trying to enhance specific sounds. You'll be quite lucky to come across an old Watkins Copicat in good condition now, though. They're quite highly prized by connoisseurs and often fetch quite a few hundred pounds. Again, a cheaper option can be computer audio plugins such as the WatKat or the Echo Cat – digital clones of the old Copicats.

The use of echo on recordings is a bit of a specialist art, really. The best way of learning how much, or how little to use is, as always, to experiment. As a lo-fi guy, however, I generally advise starting off by using way more echo than you need, before backing it off to a more sensible and listenable level. A properly trained sound engineer might possibly disagree. Good.

BACK TO HOME RECORDING

I visited a proper recording studio recently. It had a full-size mixing desk, FX racks and an engineer to sort out the sound, so that I could get on with being a pretentious DIY tart. Better though, was that it possessed one luxury which my home recording set-up does not: proper soundproofing. Insulation from the outside world, that is.

There exists a 1741 engraving by the artist William Hogarth called *The Enraged Musician*. Here, a violinist attempting to rehearse is disturbed by a cacophony in the street below. All manner of street traders shout out their wares. While they do so, a man sounds his horn, a busker plays a hautboy (oboe) and a child thrashes a drum. It's a picture which I very much relate to.

Most of the time when I'm not writing, I'm either recording or composing music at home. The archway I work above stands on a busy-ish side street. The cars and supermarket delivery vans go back and forth. The cheery young families living either side of me come and go downstairs. When school ends, several young mums and their children often gather for a pavement chat, just across the road from me. Schoolboys passing by bounce their footballs loudly outside my window or they rumble past on skateboards. Lastly, commuters returning from London, trundle wearily by, dragging their wheelie-bags.

The noise may vary but the irritation is constant. From behind my closed window I curse them frequently. But how are they to know that I'm at work on something so brilliant, that one day it might eclipse the Beatles' 'Penny Lane'? I mustn't complain. They're only civilians. They too have lives. The working world cannot dance attendance upon my fragile genius. It's my cross and I'll bear it, okay?

Besides, I've found ways around some of the noise problems. At the busiest times of day I'll work in headphones, recording electric guitars and basses directly into the desk. I mainly leave the vocals for early afternoon, which is a quieter time. Provided that nobody's sanding a floor, hammering, or road-drilling, which they often are, a bit of extraneous noise can be passed off as 'ambience'. Home-recording technology is marvellous these days. Long gone are times of soundproofing a garage with eggboxes, building a chip-board drum booth or, on a humbler level, promising your mum or the neighbours that you'll be done by 6pm.

Recording my upright piano, however, has been a constant problem. In addition to the natural street ambience, my floorboards creak. Every chair in the house creaks, the piano keys themselves click and squeak – often in untraceable places. Oh and certain bass chords sometimes set up a sympathetic rattle in other instruments. It drives me nuts. One day I did allow myself the luxury of booking a large professional recording studio which I discovered only a few miles away from my home. It had a good grand piano. In a couple of hours, I was able to record my piano parts cleanly, put them onto a memory stick and then add them to my master recording at home. It was nice, with a quality song, to take a brief holiday from lo-fi recording. In the end, though, I still prefer the wild frontier of home recording.

In earlier days, I'd spent months of my life in studios. I loved it, being locked away from the world, not even knowing what time of day it was. All of this in the company of sterling fellows just like myself – obsessed, borderline spectrum studio-rats, only interested in getting the recording down. During the 1990s, as home-recording technology improved and became cheaper, the golden age of the studio rat waned. Access to digital technology, for many hard-up musicians, was a godsend, enabling them to have multitracking facilities in their own homes.

But the technology soon superseded the art-form. This fact made many songwriters lazy. Creativity itself gradually began to boil down to how many presets you had on your new electronic toys. Since the digital cut'n'paste revolution has happened, very few stars of the Autotune Age now walk into a studio with a batch of fully formed songs. They tend, instead, to get a few half-cooked ideas, then expect the producer and the studio to weld it all up into something vaguely chart-worthy.

Songwriting, as it once was – as Rodgers and Hart, Lennon and McCartney, Carole King, and the Gershwins may have understood it – has largely degenerated into a Preset Pie, topped with cliché and nursery rhyme. The megastar singer Adele may be a recent exception. Okay, she's not Amy Winehouse, but she can at least write a song. The song 'Million Years Ago', from 2015 is a case in point. However, I do mischievously urge you to listen to a 1966 Charles Aznavour song called 'Yesterday When I Was Young'. Please don't write in.

Instead, let's move on to see how it all worked yesterday, when Newell was young. Firstly, the tunesmith and the wordsmith wrote the song. The agent took the song to a publisher. The publisher ran it around the record company. The A&R man matched the song to an artiste. An arranger sorted out the backing, while a producer told the musicians and singer how to perform it. The recording engineer got it down on tape, the record company mastered, pressed and promoted it and finally, in a best-case scenario, the public bought it. Sometimes, almost as an afterthought, the songwriters were paid.

The difference, nowadays? The internet has eaten everything. Most of the jobs I've mentioned no longer exist, while songwriting has become a curious old pastime, like sedan-chair upholstery or gibbet-building. Popular songs are now probably the worst-crafted and least memorable that they have ever been. Never have so many listened to so much, so cheaply, and got so little back. If you don't want to know the score, don't pay anyone to write it.

Home-recordists might be wondering which recording machinery the author favours. Without product placement or brazen advertising, I have to say that the majority of Cleaners from Venus works were initially recorded using a sound-on-sound method, in mono on a Sony TC630. This machine is now pretty much obsolete, but it's where I began in the distant spring of 1974.

A few years later I got the Teac/Tascam 144. This was the original 4-track Portastudio Mk 1. It ran on a cassette format and is rightfully regarded as the Ford Model T of modern DIY recording. When I'd finally exhausted my first Tascam 144, did I replace it with the new improved Tascam 244? Of course not, I went out and bought another 144. Because I knew it.

The techies who invent these devices are wonderful human beings, I'm sure. But we chowder-heads down here on Flat Earth, usually only want more of the machine that it's already taken us a year to master.

One day, my good friend Captain Sensible was kind enough to leave me, on a very long loan, a beast called the Tascam Studio 8. This was a recorder integrated into a mixer. It ran not on cassette tape but on quarter-inch tape. It had SMPTE (a time-coding feature) and each of its eight channels had three-band parametric EQ. The Captain informed me later that the aforementioned EQ was better than the mixer he was using on his new Fostex B16.

Meanwhile, back at my recording room, the Studio 8, next to the Tascam 144, seemed like the space age. It took me a bit of time to learn the features, mind. But we ended up making the Brotherhood of Lizards' *Lizardland* album on it and it does still sound good. The Studio 8 also weighed a hernia-inducing 38kg or just over five-and-a-half stones, so it wasn't actually a portastudio.

In the early 1990s, however, there came a time where my success as a poet and spoken-word artist took precedence over my music. During this period, if I needed to make a record, I mostly used other people's home recording set-ups, including Andy Partridge's shed studio, my long-term friend Nelson's home studio and my good friend Tai Chi Dave's Boss portable 8-track. I was mostly making solo albums for Cherry Red records at this time. It wasn't until about 2011, that the dormant volcano which had been the Cleaners from Venus began to rumble and smoke again. That's when I returned to DIY recording. Initially I'd only needed a tiny 4-track unit which I was using for recording jingles and station idents for a local community radio station.

After a bit of research, I discovered that good old Tascam had come up with a tiny little 4-track digital recorder, with two built-in mics. It was called the Pocketstudio. It cost somewhere round about £100 and so I bought one for my radio work.

Reader, it was a slippery slope. Soon enough the thought occurred. "I wonder what would happen if I tried to make a whole album on this thing?" To cut to the chase, after buying more instruments, widgets and cables, my living room was beginning to look pretty silly: full of music gear all centred upon a 6x4-inch box with two jack-sockets in the back.

By this time, I'd made six new Cleaners from Venus albums and it was almost 2018. I now had a manager and a US distribution deal. It eventually percolated through to me that it was about time I got myself a proper man's Portastudio. So I bought the Tascam DP03SD – an 8-track. I'm now on my second one. It means that I can make modern digital recordings, using production values first minted in 1967/1968. This was when the engineers at Abbey Road first synched up two Studer 4-track machines, for greater multi-tracking facilities. I won't bore you with how this was done but it changed music. Personally, I believe that 8-track was probably as good it ever got for pop music. So I went back there to find out why. I'm still doing the research. I may be some time.

LESSON 5
DON'T THROW THE KITCHEN SINK IN THE MIX

I guess the tip here, once again, is that old cliché that sometimes more really is less. Nowadays, Tascam and several other manufacturers make home-recording machines which give us almost infinite multitracking facilities. It's possible now to get Tascam 24-track and even 32-track machines for a reasonable price. But I've held back from buying one so far. This is because I believe that we need to make production decisions as we go along. It's what I do with my 8-track machine. I feel that if I recorded everything and the kitchen sink, before I mixed my masterpiece, that it would be a real sonic ball-of-string to deal with whenever it came to mixdown.

To have to mix your drum beat, your extra drums, your percussion and even your bass onto two or three of your tracks, will also force you into some very hard decisions. But when it's done, it's done. You will now have five or six tracks left for all the other stuff. Doing these sub-mixes as you go along will allow you to look at the end result more objectively. This ensures that you're not bogged down in daft nit-picky questions like "Is the tambourine too loud?"

Because you made that production decision way back down the road, you can't fiddle with it now. Instead, ask yourself how the actual song is sounding. Holistically, I mean. Is it working?

Essentially, I suppose I'm trying to make a cage for myself in which to be brilliant. I believe that having too much choice and too many facilities in the way of the end product is like running a fog machine in front of yourself. The last thing you need when you're finally in sight of your final mix, is to have to worry about the minutiae. Besides, even if you've got it wrong, it's not the end of the world. You may have to start all over again. But at least you'll know, second time around, what 'not' to do and what you 'don't' want. And very often, I've found, when you are forced do a total re-make, it will usually only take you half the time of your first attempts.

BLOODY BORING WAFFLE ABOUT SPEAKERS AND CANS

If you're getting speakers for your home or your home studio, don't go agonising about it too much. Just go onto the internet and find something for about 40 or 50 quid a pair. Take a look at some of the reviews by the civilians – those ordinary listeners with relatively undamaged hearing and scant pretensions. Take no notice whatsoever of the kind of speccy, bearded waffle written by hi-fi bores. Go for what the ordinary punters consider a bargain.

As for the speccy-techies: I came across an entire page of such people slagging off the very brand of speakers that I've been using happily for at least five years. Even if you do want some high-class speakers, unless you're a teetotalling, clean-living music lover with above-average hearing, you'll be pissing in the wind.

The last thing a lo-fi hero needs is great speakers. Your mission, should you choose to accept it, is to get your home-recorded masterwork sounding good on any speakers. So you don't want to be picking up too much detail. But you will need to know where the vocal is sitting in the mix.

The best way of doing this is to leave the track playing in the recording room, at a reasonable volume, before going out into the corridor or the room next door, to find out whether it sounds clearer from there. When I worked in Tin Pan Alley's 24-track studio in Denmark Street in the mid-1980s I called this method the Tin Pan Alley Toilet Test. I would leave the heavy studio door open and stand down the corridor just outside the bog. If I could hear the vox okay, I'd give it the thumbs up. If I couldn't, we'd either add a bit of treble to it, or nudge the volume up a bit.

These were the days of the old Yamaha NS-10 speakers, beloved of engineers then because of their 'colourless' sound. I hated them with a vengeance, preferring Auratones – which you won't see so often nowadays. They still exist and usually cost over £300, which is somewhat out of the home-recording remit. I'm still tempted because I love them. But even if I did get some Auratones, I'd also probably need to use some humble desktop computer speakers for a second reference. Because it's exactly such speakers that many of your listeners will be hearing your masterpiece on.

If you're making old-fashioned pop songs, you really do need to hear that vocal. Years ago, the French used to be much better at this aspect of record production than we Brits were. I worked with a French producer called Louis Philippe. Every single track on the album we made together had a noticeably more audible vocal on it. I mean, you don't want to diminish a good backing track, do you? But ever since I worked with Louis, I try to make sure that within the final mix, the lead vocal is sticking up over the pyjama elastic – so to speak.

Back to the cheaper ranges of speakers. A very great former Abbey Road studio engineer called Neil Brockbank once patiently explained to me how one's hearing may be adversely affected by even a small amount of alcohol. This was why he didn't drink when working. "Not even a half pint," he told me. Now I don't know about you, but I've found that a substantial amount of pop listeners like to enjoy a drink, or sometimes other mood enhancing aids, while they listen – especially in a party situation.

With this in mind, therefore, what is the point of getting all trainspotter-fussy about your speakers, when you know that many people just want some sonic wallpaper while they drink, yell and get off with each other?

Personally, like Neil Brockbank, I never drink while recording music these days. But I do come back from the pub sometimes and re-play whatever it is that I've been working on during the day. It's always illuminating. Sometimes it's not good, but it does give you a different overview. So, if you don't like what you're hearing following a relaxing drink, don't interfere with it now, but do make a quick note. Then, first thing the next morning, reassess the recording. Incidentally, listening back to your latest work very first thing in the day is always the best time for your objectivity. At least, I've found it to be so. Giving your ears a rest is always good.

Apart from all of this, though, I repeat: if your homemade music can be made to sound good on relatively cheap or adequate speakers, then it will probably sound just as good, if not better, on more expensive ones.

LESSON 6
THINK OF YOUR EARS

When buying headphones, or 'cans' as some call them, maybe spend a little bit more time reading the punter reviews. Again, don't pay too much attention to the audio mags but do give them a glance if they don't seem too boring. Get some cans that suit you. I prefer closed-back headphones, myself. You can spend £300 or £400 on your cans, but I usually budget somewhere between £40 and £80. Sony tend to be my faves but my current most-used ones are an Audio Technica set, which cost about £50. They were recommended to me as being good for their price – and they are. It's worth having an extra pair of cans too, with one of those widgets that allow you to plug two pairs into a mini-jack socket. Then, if you're recording a guest player or session singer, you, the recordist and they, the performer, can work in headphones together.

Your headphones do need to be a bit better than your speakers – but not so good that they make the speakers sound disappointing when you get them off your head. The chief point here is to buy good budget speakers but be prepared to spend a little more on your headphones. Shop around well and you should be able to bring it all in under about £150-£200.

My forty-quid cans
a bit worn on the
leatherette pads

MY GUITARS

It was my first electric guitar. A second-hand 1961 Hofner V3 – a solid body, with a sunburst finish. Bought in autumn 1970 in Shaftesbury Avenue, London, it cost me £19. Cheap, even for that time, it wouldn't have been of much interest to a would-be Hendrix or Clapton. German-made, it was the type of guitar once popular with instrumental bands like the Shadows or the Ventures. In other words, it was good for twangy-jangly stuff rather than for heroic guitar solos.

But I still have it. Because it has its own distinctive sound, more redolent of early-to-mid period Beatles than of Seventies axe heroes. It's very much a working guitar, which I've used on many records, preferring it to rather posher Gibsons and Fenders. My Hofner has possibly survived all this time (well, with only one serious re-build) because I've rarely used it for live shows. The only other person I know of who also owns one is Chris Rea. A Hofner V3 was his first guitar too and, like me, he's hung onto it. In a spooky coincidence, I discovered that Chris also has the same birthday as me, although he's two years older.

Men will sometimes get very strange and somewhat precious about their guitars. They like to hold detailed conversations about them in pubs, sometimes, trying to out-do each other with their technical knowledge. Some men like to hang their guitars up around the walls or stand them upright in racks, so that the living room begins to resemble a guitar shop. Women aren't always keen on this. You tend, therefore, to find the guitar-rack trait more common in men who now live by themselves.

Some men will talk authoritatively about this or that instrument, sometimes referring to a particularly treasured model as "this bad boy". I must know something about the subject, but I do try to avoid getting bogged down in such exchanges. The Hofner V3 is my most-used electric guitar. My least-used guitar is a Rickenbacker 12-string 330 model which I acquired some years ago. Rickenbacker 12-strings were favoured by the Beatles, the Byrds and the Smiths. Johnny Marr of the Smiths bought his Rickenbacker 330 from Roxy Music's Phil Manzanera, who, in turn, claimed that he acquired it from Roger McGuinn of legendary US folk-rockers, the Byrds. Apocryphal this story may be, but the guitar has now become, in legend at least, a sort of musical Excalibur.

The highly distinctive chime of a Ricky 12-string makes it a bit of a boy's toy. It's not a very versatile guitar, however. Like a beautiful vintage car that languishes un-driven in the garage for 362 days of the year, it's hugely admired, if not practical for general purposes. Shoulder-wrenchingly heavy, it needs careful tuning and is an absolute bugger to re-string. I usually set aside at least a long morning for the task. Shown off in the right place, however, it won't merely turn heads but at the sound of it, the very creatures of the forest will run around mad with joy, while all of the town's children follow after its player. out through the gates of town and over the hills, never to return.

Sitting demurely in an old photo with my Hofner V3 and the Rickenbacker 330, is a slim, rather elegant-looking violin bass. A year or two ago, after I'd managed to afford a genuine Hofner violin bass. I gave the first one away to Wix and Wrabness Primary School whom I considered to be in need of such a thing

That first bass looked very much like the Hofner violin model made famous by Paul McCartney. It was actually a Westfield copy. The Westfield was almost as good as an original Hofner but possibly possessed more reliable electrics than some of the originals. I bought it because I was in a hurry and needed a cheap bass for some live work that I was then doing. I initially thought that for the price, it must have been a Chinese-made guitar. To my surprise I discovered that Westfield was actually a Scottish firm. A blooming good one too, until they went out of business in 2013.

Much to the disgust of manlier fellows, I opted for this violin bass, not just because it was cheap but because I thought it looked pretty. I also got a nice Sixties sound out of it when I was recording. The Westfield was capable of producing a pleasing boxiness. It had something of the scout-hut about it, perfect for a lo-fi guy like me. I used it on many of my records too and it stood up to quite a lot.

My knowledge of guitars doesn't extend to much more than basic maintenance and a bit of Mr Sheen spray polish. With basses I mostly don't change their strings from one year to the next. And if they ever need fixing I take them to a techie who knows about that sort of stuff. My most recent electric guitar acquisition was my long-desired Hofner Verithin. It's a dark cherry model with a feedback-reducing centre-block and modern electrics. Not very ambitious by some standards, I know, but I just love Hofners – my whole musical life has been bound up with them.

LESSON 7
YOU DON'T ALWAYS NEED AN AMP

Now this may either surprise you or appall you, but I've hardly ever used an amplifier when recording guitars. The only time I can remember doing so was when I was making my first proper album *Barricades and Angels* (1980) with a band called the Stray Trolleys. We were recording a song called 'Love Into Action' and it needed a sort of 1966-style rock solo. To my slight alarm, the guitarist Max Volume – a brilliant player in most cases – announced to me that he "didn't really do solos", but that I was welcome to use his guitar.

Since there were no effects pedals, I got the guitar – I think it was a Gibson (and I can't remember which model) – and bunged it through an amp and speaker (and I can't remember what kind of amp). I cranked the fucker up so it was on the edge of howling and we miked it with an SM57, I think. The engineer, Dave Hoser, returned to the control room and rolled the tape. I took one run at it and threw every rock'n'roll cliché I knew at it, with Hoser yelling "Keep playing!" through the cans at me. The curious may care to search for 'Love Into Action' by the Stray Trolleys. The results can be heard between 2m19s and about 2m58s. So, I ran into the control room half-deafened, in order to have a listen. It was passable. "Have to fuckin' do, wunnit?" I said. Four decades later, it does actually sound okay.

Only months later, while recording with the Cleaners from Venus for the first time, I found what would become 'the sound of the Cleaners' – if there is such a thing. Using my un-trustworthy Hofner V3, I plugged the guitar firstly into a Frontline compressor pedal. I then linked that to an MXR pedal. I set this to a sort of mild chorus effect with the regeneration pot turned down to zero. I linked this into a 1979 Watkins Copicat echo unit. I then plugged the whole ensemble into the recording machine. During the entire Cleaners DIY years, I don't think I ever recorded guitars using an amplifier. The sound at which I was aiming was a sort of cross between early Hank Marvin and mid-period George Harrison. No idea whether I succeeded, but I liked the sound I got and am still using something similar to this day. So I'm the wrong guy to ask about miking-up guitars in the studio, because I've never done it.

There is one piece of advice here, though. When using this method, it's probably best to work in headphones. Not too loud either because it can get tiring on the ears. So, after about an hour, if you're still not getting what you want, give your ears and yourself a break and leave it for an hour or two. Or come back to it in the morning. Recording electric guitars in this fashion can be among the best and worst things in the world. Carry on, then.

My favourite talent booster
pedal — after the WEM Copicat

£19.00 Hofner V3 — Guitar Village
Shaftesbury Avenue — Oct. 1970

ONLY THE SHADOWS KNOW

A few years ago, and what with everything else going on in 2020, I'd almost forgotten about the Shadows. A tick and five gold stars therefore, to the BBC, who, decades after the event, screened a terrific hour-long documentary *The Shadows at Sixty*. As a lifelong fan of the Shads, I couldn't fault the documentary and I even learned stuff about the band that I hadn't known previously. The Shadows were the first British pop group prior to the Beatles with some kind of universal appeal. I cannot recall anyone ever saying, "I never really liked the Shadows."

They were perfect for boys like me who, then aged eight or nine, were keen on pop music but didn't like any of that soppy singing about love. Nope, the Shadows were great because they played heroically upbeat, twangy guitar instrumentals. It was the kind of music which went perfectly with sunny Saturday mornings, when there was no school, you'd just received your pocket money and the world belonged to you.

The Shadows (without Cliff Richard) notched up their first hit 'Apache' in the late summer of 1960. 'Apache', in fact, was sitting at Number One in the charts around about the time that an unknown teenage quartet called the Beatles were beginning their third week's work in Hamburg. George Harrison would later say, "If it hadn't been for the Shadows there would have been no Beatles."

The Shads were a peculiarly British construction. Their nearest American contemporaries were the Ventures, who, although there was some overlap in the choice of tunes, never seemed quite as smart or as exciting as the Shads. The melodies of some of the early Shadows hits were frequently beautiful – and beautifully arranged. Tunes like 'Apache' and 'Wonderful Land' were written by Jerry Lordan, a one-time comedian-singer who'd developed a knack for songwriting. It's a curious thing that despite the epic qualities of his tunes, Lordan was said to have demoed them using not a guitar but a ukulele. The members of the Shadows themselves, however, were no slouches and soon developed into formidable tunesmiths.

Hank Marvin and Bruce Welch, a couple of Geordie grammar-school lads, took the train from Newcastle to London in 1958 and never looked back. They became Cliff Richard's backing band and, following a line-up change, were joined by Brian Bennett, resident drummer at Soho's famous 2i's Café – along with bassist Brian 'Licorice' Locking. When, in 1962, Cliff and the band were asked to write a few songs for the musical film *Summer Holiday*, they excelled themselves, composing the title song, as well as 'Bachelor Boy', 'Foot Tapper' and a number of other stand-out tunes. The *Observer* newspaper voted the film the best musical of 1962 and, as the royalties flooded in, one or two of the band members went out and bought themselves Rolls-Royces.

The Shadows by this time were a band absolutely at the top of their game. Decades later, one of the salient things about them is that there's none of the standard rock'n'roll clag attached to them – no sex, drug scandals or bust-ups. Nor is there much more personal tragedy in the story than there would have been with anyone else who'd been on the planet for almost 80 years. The Shadows' star-time as a band was, strictly speaking, between about mid-1960 and 1967. Considering that pop-music fashions moved at warp-speed during this era, they did brilliantly. If they were briefly under the pop radar during the decade between psychedelia and punk, at no time can I recall anyone ever deriding them as has-beens. Genuinely popular, the Shadows were and still are regarded with huge respect and deep affection.

In 1977, however, somewhere deep within the goes-around-comes-around world of showbiz, something rather odd happened. The year was one of industrial unrest and political dissatisfaction in the UK. With punk rock and disco doing battle for the soundtrack of that era, the last thing anyone expected was a Shadows revival. Until, that is, someone at EMI records decided that now was time to release the Shadows *20 Golden Greats*. Around this time there was a music business in-joke about EMI. It went, "What's the difference between EMI and the *Titanic*?" The answer was, "The *Titanic* had a good band."

20 Golden Greats arrived with rather an austere sleeve design. There wasn't even a picture of the lads: just a silhouette of three guitar necks against a bare wall. It came in a particular shade – a sort of backstreet boozer nicotine-yellow colour. There was however an unforgettable TV ad campaign, featuring a chap in sleeveless pullie, standing in his bedroom, miming to the Shadows hits with his cricket bat. Suddenly, everyone remembered. The album went straight into the charts and sat there at Number One for six weeks. I still have my original cassette. On the back sleeve it says, rather poignantly, 'Also available on 8-track cartridge.' Apart from that, however – and the Beatles – as a record label, what else did EMI ever do?

LESSON 8
DON'T JUMP ON THE BANDWAGON

As the financial product brochures always warn you, 'Shares may go down as well as up.' This too, is often (although not always) the case with music trends. The Shadows, who kicked off the beat-boom right at the outset of the 1960s, seemed almost 'safe' by mid-1964, after the Beatles and the Stones had established themselves. In music fashion the turnover is fast and the public are fickle. And yet almost every kind of music – even Glam Rock, where I started – gets a second chomp at the apple, if only for irony's sake. Music that was really good in the first place, however, like the Shadows' material, will often wake some youthful memory in people's hearts. There will always be a place in the world's affections for the cheery music of the Shads. So, whichever genre of music plucks you out of obscurity, only to throw you back there later, don't worry. Get on with something new and keep an eye out for a revival – even if it's only a revival of one song. Because it's not over till it's over. And sometimes, not even then.

ON THE BUS WITH CLIFF

The Observer called it 'The most cheerful and skilful British musical of our generation'. *Summer Holiday*, first shown in British cinemas early in 1963, starred Cliff Richard and the Shadows, Una Stubbs, Ron Moody, Melvyn Hayes and David Kossoff. Interesting too, if not so well-known, is the fact that the film's depiction of Yugoslavians as hapless peasants had angered Marshall Tito enough for him to ban Cliff Richard and the film's director, Peter Yates, from that country for life. In the UK during the summer of 1962, when the film was being made, Cliff Richard and the Shadows were the UK's top pop stars. The Beatles back then were still only an approaching jangle from a distant northern province. By the time of the film's release, changes were becoming apparent, however.

Up until 1963, the average career-minded pop singer might enjoy a couple of years of stardom before attempting the transition to 'all-round entertainer'. With two films already on his CV, Cliff was well on-track. *Summer Holiday* leaned very much towards a traditional musical style. Although many of the show's 16 tunes were penned by show-veterans Pete Myers and Ronnie Cass, its two flagship songs, 'Summer Holiday' and 'Bachelor Boy' were written by members of the Shadows and Cliff himself. Stanley Black, the film's musical director, must have been an adventurous helmsman to have allowed free rein to such diverse songwriting teams. It was their combination, however, which helped make the film a hit. Almost six decades later, it remains a winning blend of youthful Sixties optimism and standard showbiz schmaltz.

The song 'Bachelor Boy', was a last-minute entry. The production crews had already returned to the UK when the Shadows got in touch to announce that they'd written this terrific new song. The now-famous scene with the London bus and that daft skipping dance which accompanied 'Bachelor Boy', was therefore filmed, not in Greece, but in an Elstree studio, hastily mocked up to look vaguely Hellenic – which was only a partial success. You could say that the story was corny, not very rock'n'roll and above all, unfeasible.

The plot? Four young bus mechanics decide to convert a London double-decker bus into a sort of live-in caravan which they'll drive across Europe as a prototype continental holiday. If it works, they reason, they may be able to develop the idea as a holiday business, with a fleet of similarly converted buses. Ah, but they reckon without 1) a famous teenage American singer as their stowaway, along with 2) her conniving mother, and 3) Do Re Mi, a trio of female singers whose car has broken down en route to a residency in an Athens nightclub. Consequently, all manner of adventures and mishaps ensue, as well as lots of singing, dancing and yes, a big romance between the Bachelor-Boy-in-Chief and the US lurve interest, played by Lauri Peters. As a personal footnote here, I'd just like to say that I'd have chosen the unutterably lovely Una Stubbs over Lauri Peters any time, but then that's entirely subjective.

If you are a Shadows fan, however, this film is for you. In 1962 the band were absolutely at the top of their game. If, conversely, you are a fan of London buses, this film may also be for you. And yes, I know that the bus featured here isn't a Routemaster but one of its predecessors – the much-missed AEC Regent III RT. Now, go away and please don't write in.

To sketch in some historical detail here, only 18 years before *Summer Holiday* was made, Europe was still at war. Since, in 1962 the package holiday hadn't become what we modernists now call 'a thing', groups of young lads didn't usually go off together gallivanting across Europe – unless, of course, it was felt by the prevailing British government that someone over there had lately been getting above himself (again) and needed a quiet word.

The bus route that Cliff took from London to Athens, was almost the same as the one which your young correspondent later took in the 1970s, on a somewhat less-fragrant hippy bus from London Victoria to Piraeus Harbour in Greece. The trip took in bits of France, Germany and Austria, before a long haul across the former Yugoslavia, over the Macedonian mountains and into Greece. I bet none of Cliff's party were hauled off the bus and searched as often as I was, although they did have to dodge a bit of gunfire.

To British cinema audiences struggling through the late winter slush of early 1963, the dazzling Aegean skies, the skimpy clothes and the cheerful danciness of *Summer Holiday* must have seemed irresistible. Then, to emerge from the cinema into the chilly late winter air and to hear 'Please Please Me' spilling from nearby cafés might have alerted them to the changes on the way. Prophetically, early on in the film, as the London bus first hoves into view, within less than ten seconds everything fades up from 1950s monochrome into (almost) glorious Eastmancolor. Within a year or two it would all happen in real life.

LESSON 9
TOURING ISN'T REALLY A 'CREATIVE JOURNEY'

Despite the fact that I am much travelled, it occurs to me that with the new technology, many modern musicians shouldn't feel obliged to go touring. In fact, with the advent of holograms, touring could probably end altogether. A very famous band playing Wembley Stadium, for instance, isn't really offering much in the way of real value, other than giving audience members the dubious privilege of being able to say afterwards, "I was there." All that most audience members will be able to see are the giant moving images of their heroes splayed upon the huge screens mounted around the stadium. The actual band members themselves will appear, to the majority of audience members, as a group of expensively lit ants.

Now, some people may regard this sort of thing as 'good value'. This is for a ticket which cost somewhere in three-figures. They will talk effusively about the 'atmosphere'. Of course they will. What else could they say? "I just paid £300 for two of us to travel to London then stand in a football ground watching and listening to some expensively lit ants?" Well I wouldn't do it. Nor would I ever agree to play any large event where I and all the audience members could not make eye contact with each other.

The main thing I noticed about gigs, however, is how much energy they take away from my writing and recording schedule. Songs and the recording of them are what I do best and what I prefer doing. If therefore, like me, you begin to have success with your musical creations and then someone wants to interrupt you by suggesting that you play some gigs when you don't want to, simply refuse. I usually do. If they really want you to tour, and you say no, I've found that one of three things will happen:

1. They'll stop pestering you
2. They'll offer you better venues and better money
3. They'll send a film crew to make a documentary about you.

That third option's not too bad, is it?

RESIDENTIAL PAMPERING

It was one afternoon in late April 1986 that I arrived at Ridge Farm, a residential recording studio on the Surrey-Sussex border. "Call us when you get to Dorking, we can pick you up," they offered. I declined. The studio was only about eight miles away so I cycled there from the station. A turn-off down a pretty lane and there she was – a former farmhouse, resembling more a small Elizabethan manor house.

Graham Gouldman, 10cc's bass player and one of my all-time songwriting heroes, had left the studio shortly before I arrived on my bike. The new pop star in residence at the studio, busy making his 'difficult' third album, was a member of a famous band as well as being a chartbusting solo star. He'd been working too hard, and when his muse went on her break I was one of three lyricists drafted in to assist with songwriting. It was the recording engineer, Tony Phillips, with whom I'd once been in a band, had suggested my involvement. Summoned at very short notice, I bungeed a portable typewriter onto my carrier, slung the bike in the guard's van at Colchester and rumbled off to Sussex.

What I hadn't realised was exactly how opulent this recording studio was. Queen had recorded there, as had Ozzy Osbourne, the Smiths and a number of other rock luminaries. If you've been booked in to record an entire album and the residential studio charges £1,200 a day (and this was in the mid-1980s), then you'd better not be messing around. Unless, of course, it was only an expensive working holiday that you really wanted. While intoxicated by chart success, I understand that it can be surprisingly easy to go with the latter option.

The actual recording studio was situated in a large, beautifully converted wooden barn. Its upstairs control room, which overlooked the main recording suite, resembled the flight deck of a starship. Somewhere below was a room housing all of the fans for that recording machinery, which needed to be kept cool. Importantly, here was also stored a crate or two of top-notch lager. Dinner took place each evening around a large table in the big house. A cordon-bleu cook arrived each afternoon in order to prepare exquisite dinners for us. There were always snacks and drinks on hand. After dinner, we'd return to the studio and press on into the small hours. It was just like an office job, in a way – but with more grog, fantastic cooking, beautiful surroundings, Martian working hours and exotic company.

Reality rarely intruded. Until, one afternoon, a man wandered into the house, turned on the TV and asked us, "Seen this?" In Ukraine, we learned, the Chernobyl nuclear reactor had exploded. A vast radioactive cloud, pushed by seasonal north-easterly winds, was now heading towards the UK. I'd been introduced to this man a day earlier. John 'Speedy' Keen was around the studio a lot. I never did find out why. He looked the part, however. He had a classic English rock-star face: biggish hooter, blond hair and blue eyes with a slightly artful look. He'd have fitted into any late-Sixties band you could name. A former road manager, he'd previously done a bit of driving for Pete Townshend, with whom he'd attended grammar school. Speedy was a mixer and fixer. He also played several instruments and produced records. The main thing, however, was that in 1969 he'd written and then sung on a very famous Number One hit record, 'Something in the Air' by Thunderclap Newman.

Upon first being introduced, I'd asked, "*You're Speedy Keen?*" Far more important to me was the fact that he'd written Track 1/Side 1 of *The Who Sell Out*, the first pop album that I'd ever bought. "You wrote 'Armenia City in the Sky'," I stated. He nodded. "I bet not many people tell you that." He looked at me, mock forlornly and replied "You're only the third. Ever!" There was laughter. I shook his hand. That sort of thing, for me, is the thrill of the music industry – the backroom boys and the people I met in recording studios were often more interesting than those at much glitzier places. To temper the decadent luxury of days spent in a residential studio, however, was this sombre news that because of a nuclear accident in the Ukraine we might soon be irradiated. No rose without a thorn, I supposed.

Speedy Keen died of sudden heart failure in 2002, aged 56. Chernobyl didn't quite destroy the world, as some of us had feared that it might. Tony Phillips, our recording engineer for those sessions, ended up working with Joni Mitchell and many other luminaries. He now lives in Los Angeles. Captain Sensible, the star whose album we were all working on, eventually back-burnered the solo career and returned to his much-celebrated punk band, the Damned. Now in their 60s and 70s, the Damned recently filled the Albert Hall. Led Zeppelin's Jimmy Page remains a long-time fan of the band. Ridge Farm, for two decades one of the UK's finest residential studios, quit the music business and became a reportedly wonderful wedding venue. And me? Ah, you know? I'm choogling along.

LESSON 10
HOME HAS ITS BENEFITS OVER THE 'BIG STUDIO'

From a die-hard home recordist's point of view, it's educative and sometimes fun working in a big expensive studio. If you're ever invited into one to work, or if it's not going to cost you much, you should try it. As well as Ridge Farm and Abbey Road, I've worked in a few other such places here and abroad. At the end of it all, however, I still prefer recording at home. Why? Because I'm at home, basically, and I'm not having to come up to the high standards of a trained engineer who may rear up when I ask him to make something sound a bit cheaper and nastier.

Working in chaos or improvising within set limits can sometimes elicit more pleasing results than luxuriating in technological opulence. When you're in an expensive studio and things are becoming boring or sterile, because of the money at stake, you can't just down tools and fuck off to the pub. Sometimes you get good days, sometimes you get bad days. It's nobody's fault. It's just like that. Learn to recognise a bad day and to take a 'head-break'. Get some food, some company and some sleep. It will be a better day tomorrow. However, when the clock's ticking and the meter's racking up money in a big expensive studio, you can't always do that. When you're recording at home, you can do as you wish.

DRUMFOOLERY: A PERSONAL HISTORY OF DRUMS AND PERCUSSION

Drums? I'm the wrong person to ask, really. I once spent three months of my spare time with a drum kit, attempting to play simple 4/4 beats. I couldn't manage it. Decades later I learned from someone who'd taught people with learning difficulties, that I had a condition known as 'dyspraxia'. I also can't drive a car. In addition, I couldn't wink with my left eye, or close the same eye whenever attempting to aim a rifle. At school I was useless at team games such as football. If someone shouted at me, "On your left!" it took me a while to figure out which side to go. I had to think about it before acting.

As well as drum kits, other musical instruments which I can't quite manage include accordions and bowed instruments. Yes, I can find and make the notes on such things, but what I can't do, for instance is, say, with an accordion, play the notes at one speed while operating the bellows at another.

Plucked instruments and keyboards are things with which I have little trouble, although I understand that my piano style is somewhat unconventional.

Without going into all the gobbledegook about my dyspraxia – once known as 'clumsy child syndrome' I'm told – and without going into exactly what part of the spectrum I inhabit, I have a confession. As a 10-year-old, having got the bug for pop music, I saw myself becoming a drummer. For me, it seemed the most heroic role in a pop group. Luckily for me, my parents didn't want me to have a drum kit. We compromised. On my 12th Christmas I got a six-string acoustic guitar.

In my early years as the singer and occasional guitarist in my first groups, I rarely went near the drums – because I knew that I couldn't even hold down a simple in-time beat. It was only when I got that first Sony tape recorder with sound-on-sound, a very basic multi-tracking facility, that I began to explore how drums and percussion worked.

In my early home recording days, sometimes using a nearby alarm clock as my click track, I'd put down a bass-drum beat by banging the heel of my hand for three minutes on a wooden floor. I also discovered that a tambourine was very useful for driving a song. I went through all the usual experiments with kitchen percussion too. Knitting needles on shoeboxes were good. Split-peas in a long plastic jar for shakers. Dried peas in other smaller vessels for maracas etc. I even figured out how to make an electric snare sound, by pegging a sheet of kitchen foil to a clothes drying rack in the bath and then spraying short beats at it with a plant-spray jet. Enough of these objects, in various combinations, could create some sort of beat-with-percussion for my first recordings. Even by DIY standards, however, they were a little ersatz.

My problem with drummers was not, as the standard clichés suggest, that they weren't very bright. Nearly always it was quite the opposite. In at least two bands I've been in, the drummer was the most academically high-achieving person present. My main problem, with some drummers anyway, was that I couldn't get them to simply play one moronic beat for me. I always felt I'd be insulting their intelligence. I also didn't know the necessary terminology to actually tell them what I wanted. In the early days I wouldn't have known how to ask for a blues shuffle, a march, a four-to-the-floor rock-thrash or a Seventies disco beat with a closed hi-hat on the off-beat. As a young singer, such things were not in my lexicon.

Many drummers have a certain amount of natural mathematical logic. I, however, am a mathematical dummy. I really am. I had to have remedial lessons at school. I hated them. So I left school. Many of the best drummers are interested in the complexities of funk or jazz and will often want to put cross-rhythms and myriad other distractions into a part. They've learned the chops, so naturally they want to use them in the song.

But I'm not interested in anything like that. What I liked about Lol Elliott, who co-founded the Cleaners from Venus as a drummer, was his lack of frills and fuss. He'd usually put down a simple and very natural sounding beat, occasionally throwing in the odd tom fills, while I improvised a bass part around it. I found him very easy to work with and so I lost some of my awkwardness about working with drummers. The two of us often added extra percussion together, dubbing it all live via the WEM Copicat Echo machine – drums, bass and much else. It was a glorious shambles and such fun. I usually built the rest of the track around whatever came out of it. Most of what we recorded, we used. Our technique would have appalled more accomplished musicians and engineers. That's why it was such fun.

When Lol left the Cleaners a year or two later to be with his girlfriend who lived 200 miles away, I was bereft – not to mention stumped for what to do next. So I bought a cheap and very basic drum machine – a Sound Master SR-88.

I began to use this and, variously, fed it through spring reverb, flanger and compression pedals – just to see what would happen. Well, it didn't sound any more like a proper drum kit, but it did make some interesting sounds in its own right. I'd also combine it with kitchen percussion, along with a real Premier tom-tom and an old sizzle cymbal which I'd acquired. Although I didn't know it at the time, this combining of sounds from the over-processed SR-88, along with real, or kitchen percussion, became the drum sound of the early Cleaners from Venus.

Over the next two or three years, Lol Elliott returned occasionally for a weekend, whereupon I'd borrow a drum kit from someone, then persuade him to record some beats for me while he was there. Apart from this, I struggled somewhat for my drum beats. It was all a bit hit-and-miss in the period between Lol leaving in 1982 and the very drum-savvy Giles Smith joining in 1985. It took me a long time to realise that, actually, I'd created a drum and rhythm sound of my own, which others would come to regard as perfectly valid, long before I ever believed in it myself.

So here was the lesson. With drums and percussion, anything and everything is valid. It took rap and hip-hop, and the world's gradual acceptance of lo-fi, to teach me this. Being the age I am (a Sixties child and early teenager) I believed that to make pop music, you needed a proper drummer. Coming into my teens, I experienced all the self-importance of prog rock descending from its pompous mountain. Various groups of young men, some of whom had benefited from a musical education, decided to make pop music more complex and weighty, perhaps to endow it with a validity that would help it to be taken more seriously. LPs, now referred to as 'albums' took priority over singles. Songs became 'numbers' or 'pieces'. It was middle-class pseudo-intellectual bollocks in many cases. Luckily, not too much of it troubled the pop charts.

I was a pop fan, basically. I liked three-minute singles. I had no pretentions or desire to 'validate' pop as a serious art form. In my teens I thought classical music was the music of the enemy and that jazz was for speccy bearded bores. Between the ages of 15 and 20 I just wanted singles by the Who, the Move, the Small Faces and groups like that. Everyone else, as far as I was concerned, could just fuck off.

In 1967-68, Ginger Baker – actually a jazz drummer and a bloody good one – became the industry standard. Sure, he was great but he just wasn't pop. Kenney Jones, Keith Moon and Ringo Starr were pop. Charlie Watts was pop and jazz. But Charlie wasn't showy with it. He was just sort of... well, perfect, really. In the 1970s, a famous jazz drummer called Buddy Rich announced that rock drummers were only rock drummers because they couldn't play jazz. Well, technically brilliant as he may have been I wouldn't want Buddy Rich playing on my records. Way too over-the-top. From a drummer I just require the beat and a few surprises in unexpected places. As I said, I came of age just at a time when the pretentious twats were starting to over-analyse pop. That was where the rot set in.

Luckily, in the late 1970s and early 80s, punk rock came along. It was closely followed by DIY, rap and hip-hop. If punk was the sound of pop music 'refreshing itself' by showering off all the clagginess of prog, then DIY, rap and hip-hop were the sounds of a new generation dancing to their own new drums. It was drum-anarchy. They used cheap beatboxes, bass drums without snares, drum loops, industrial samples, processed handclaps and much else. What they sometimes didn't use were actual drummers.

Finally, the digi-tide swept over us. By now you could buy software and make up your own composite digital drummer, using almost any beat with any kit – past, present or future. But I'm chiefly talking about recording music here. So don't worry, drummers. As long as there are bands, be they indie, blues, Americana, or tribute bands, you'll always be watched and loved – usually by other drummers who wish that they were up there instead of you.

LESSON 11
THERE ARE NO STRICT RULES WITH DRUMS

Don't be afraid to use cheap drum sounds. If you have a guitar pedal with a small beatbox incorporated, try using it for the main beat of your track, then dub other percussive sounds onto it later for the 'cake decoration'. If you have a decent drum machine, but you don't like how metronomic it sounds, use a basic beat and then over-dub some of the toms and extra cymbals by hand. The bits you add will be slightly out-of-time, a thing which may re-humanise the beat somewhat. Mix and match are the watchwords here. As well as putting unsuitable amounts of reverb on the drums (if only to see what happens), try recording a straight 4/4 beat absolutely flat without reverb. It can be interesting to hear what happens when the singer sounds like they're in Canterbury cathedral and the drummer sounds like he's sitting on the sofa next to your gran while she's knitting.

I thought for years that there were strict rules to do with drums and drumming, along with some kind of mystique attached to how they fitted in with the song. This was a myth, probably one which was spread by drummers. There are no rules. Do what sounds good to you. Do as much or as little as you think you can get away with. And don't forget, sometimes the best drum kit in the house may be found in the kitchen.

Ah— my first non-human drummer. Made motorbike noises when sped up

HOW I WROTE A NEW NATIONAL ANTHEM

In early 2002, a campaign group, in conjunction with an independent English brewery, launched a competition to write a new national anthem. The opinion, long-held in some quarters, that our existing national anthem *God Save The King* is a terrible dirge, was one I subscribed to. Great Britain, the breezy island nation which spawned me, is known for producing good poets and songwriters. Why then, do we continue to sing our current national anthem, with its threnody of a tune and its archaic lyrics?

Do we need a national anthem? Some might say not. I think, however, that we probably do need one. We need it for sports matches and certain other recreational events. We also need something that can act as a signature tune-cum-soundtrack for our tourist industry: a tune to evoke the beauty of our coastlines, along with that patchwork quilt of fields, downlands and wooded hills which comprise our well-loved countryside. We deserve something stirring, pastoral and beautiful. *God Save The King* suggests only crumbling castles, defunct empires, rusty old cannons and antiquated plumbing.

I can't remember how or where I heard of the new national anthem competition, but I immediately applied for an entry form. I was a latecomer, however. I had only days to compose words and music which might fit the bill. Going on what I'd remembered of popular alternative anthem suggestions, the two main contenders seemed to be Gustav Holst's 'I Vow to Thee My Country' and Elgar's 'Land of Hope and Glory'. My own choice among existing tunes might have been Eric Coates' 'The Dam Busters March'. I could see however, how certain of the concerned classes might rear up at the very suggestion, perceiving it, however wrongly, as bellicose and overtly nationalistic.

In fact, 'The Dam Busters March' was composed by Coates in the mid-1950s as an exercise in imitation of Edward Elgar. Coates, reportedly, had to be cattle-prodded into letting the film's producers use his tune. Only eventually did he agree to allow use of it, acknowledging finally that it suited the film quite well. It was with Vaughan Williams, Holst, Elgar and Coates very much in mind, therefore, that I sat at my piano for most of a day slaving over a tune which I thought might work. I then spent much of the following day writing the lyrics for what became 'Lions and Wild Roses'.

Quickly dashing down a rough sketch of the piece on my tiny cassette speech-recorder, I then booked a morning session at my friend Nelson's spare-room studio.

Using two keyboard parts and one double-tracked vocal, I recorded my demo as best I could, mixed it and then cycled home. In time-honoured fashion, I packaged up the demo cassette, whacked a first-class stamp on it and then posted it to the competition holders. I wasn't expecting much. It was just a punt, that's all.

While writing the lyrics to 'Lions and Wild Roses' (currently mislaid) I remained wary of getting too gung-ho about my subject matter. I kept in mind a positive, classless image of footballers, pop musicians, engineers, fashion designers, comedians, inventors and medics. I was writing for exactly such a melting pot, people of any social class or racial heritage. They could have come from a London housing estate, an East Anglian market town, a northern fishing port, or a Birmingham suburb. But they would possess that admixture of skill, ingenuity, humour, practicality and stubbornness which some have claimed are among our national assets. Cheerfulness and youthful fortitude in the face of adversity would be the anthem's main theme, rather than the existing, "Our omnipotent deity will strongly support our even odder monarchy and we'll smash into pieces anyone who opposes this somewhat shaky concept."

I didn't, in all honesty, expect to hear anything from the competition holders. Even if I did, how likely would it be that anyone in the entire country would ever accept the idea of our lolloping old donkey of a national anthem being usurped by something new – even if it had a better tune? Ever the optimist, however, I put all thoughts of failure aside and waited.

Some days later, a letter arrived, saying that my song had been shortlisted in the competition. I phoned Nelson to give him the news. I'd done this sort of thing before, of course. I'd once won something in a regional poetry competition. Upon receiving only the news that I'd 'won a prize' I didn't bother turning up to the ceremony. The reason for this was simple. After a hard week's manual labour, the builder with whom I'd been working paid me up and suggested that we went out drinking lager together. It sounded far better than getting washed and changed then going all the way into town, only to stand with a bunch of amateur poets, before collecting £10 and a book token, or something similar.

You see, I had money in my pocket and I wanted to stand in a pub with other rough labourers getting trollied. What I didn't know, however, was that I'd won the actual competition: First Prize and Essex Poet of the Year 1988. The organisers were suitably cross when I didn't show up. In April 2002, meanwhile, soon after learning that I'd been shortlisted in the New National Anthem competition, there was an important news bulletin. Queen Elizabeth the Queen Mother had died. I never heard anything from the competition organisers again.

LESSON 12
TRY SOMETHING DIFFERENT

Entering strange competitions such as the one featured here, may not make you any money, but it can be fun and will often give you a creative experience way out of your usual musical territory. I have entered a handful of competitions in my time and have always come away from the exercise with knowledge which I wouldn't otherwise have gained.

Home recording is one long experiment. No two days are ever the same. Sure, you can keep notes, as a scientist might, in order to try to repeat recording methods which have gone well. Usually, however, you'll discover that no matter how meticulous you've been, something indefinable in your set-up will have changed by the next day. You may never get that bass sound, that guitar twang or that combination of effects again. The reverse side of this coin is that each new day is a clean page with fresh possibilities.

Do also try new forms of music, or methods of recording which you've never used before. I'd never previously attempted to compose a national anthem – or any other type of anthem for that matter. In fact, the piece of music actually came out quite well, and I learned something along the way about using cellos and French horns, which do seem to work well together. I'll conclude here by saying that about 50 per cent of everything I've ever done — at least, that which I've been pleased with — has occurred through lucky accidents or hasty experiments. So don't be afraid to take risks.

MY OLD PIANO

The first piano that I can remember, is one that was in my gran's living room. It had, so I learned, only appeared after Mollie, my mum's younger sister, had accomplished two extraordinary feats. Firstly, as a young teenager, she'd taught herself to read music. Then, she taught herself to play piano on 'borrowed' pianos – instruments in other people's houses, or pianos lying around un-played in halls or other community buildings. She did this all on her own initiative. I'd guess that this would have been during the 1940s.

The family wasn't rich. Her father, my grandad, was a bus driver and her mother was a busy housewife who took in wartime evacuees and, during peacetime, lodgers. In the mid-20th Century, in days before widespread ownership of televisions, pianos were far more frequently found in people's homes, in community halls and in pubs. But for Mollie to have taught herself sight-reading, as well as how to play a piano was, nonetheless, pretty impressive. She was an under-sized, pretty girl, who'd been so ill with rheumatic fever as a child that she couldn't attend school until she was seven. Mollie was encouraged instead to read, by her father, who himself had left school at 13. They were a working-class family who believed that if you were to improve your circumstances, you must start off by doing it for yourself. The reading of books, therefore, was to be encouraged. At some point, towards the end of the 1940s, with a bit of scrimping and saving by the family, Mollie finally got her piano.

In 1966, when I came home from Singapore, aged 13, I went to visit my aunt, who by then was living in Colchester – and there was the piano. On its sheet-music holder was the manuscript for the Moody Blues 1965 hit 'Go Now'. At this age I was only just learning the guitar. I was mightily impressed that my hip young auntie, who like my mother had married an army officer, also had this connection to my world.

About four years later, my own family, who'd now settled in the UK, were living temporarily in Mollie's Colchester house after she and her family had been posted abroad again. During the winter of 1970, now aged 17, I came home for a few months and began to tinker around on Mollie's piano. I had to do it when my father was out, because he cribbed about the noise, just as he had after I first began teaching myself guitar. But I gradually taught myself a few chords and how to change the sound of them by moving the bass notes around with my left hand. I even wrote a couple of songs. They were rudimentary and a little corny. One of them was called 'Richmond Park on a Sunday'. My mother liked it but even then I knew I still had a long way to go.

A few months earlier, Mike Wedgewood, a slightly older lad who rented the room upstairs from me in south

London's bedsitter-land, had given me an old harmonium – a type of small pedal organ once commonly found in Salvation Army halls. It was the most basic kind of keyboard in existence but I was highly delighted with it. I taught myself to play a few blues scales on it. I also learned some minor-chord progressions. If you play in the key of D minor, I discovered, you didn't need to go anywhere near the black notes. That's the level that I was at.

The harmonium droned and squeaked, while my feet clattered away on the treadles underneath the keyboard, making the bellows wheeze air into its pipes. It was the prog-rock era and organ sounds were quite fashionable at that time. It must have all sounded pretty dreadful, but at 17 I saw it as a potential gateway to my becoming the next Keith Emerson. Crude as the old harmonium was, it was pivotal to my disjointed musical education. I just didn't know it back then.

All through my confused and, er... 'troubled' teens, whenever I came across a piano which was vaguely playable, I was on it, attempting, as my auntie Mollie had done, to learn as much as I possibly could, while I possibly could. During my early 20s, the process continued, until one day in 1978, I was actually given a rather worn-out but useable piano by Tony Phillips, who played bass in my band, Gypp. It was a bit of a donkey but I was very glad to get it because, through persistence, I learned much on it.

A year or two later, my new landlord, Peter Brightmore, whom I believe had once run a side-hustle selling old pianos, sold me my current piano, a slightly battle-scarred but very good upright Steck. This would have been about

1980. I was still a hard-up kitchen porter at that time but because Peter was a very kindly bloke he allowed me to buy the instrument in instalments over a period of about a year. It changed my life. I have never been a good piano player and am never likely to be. But what the piano did for me was to give me a new and important dimension to my songwriting, one which was well beyond what I could contrive on a guitar alone.

At the time of writing, I have owned this piano for almost 45 years. The songs which I've written on it have helped me at various times to pay a mortgage, feed children, pay vets' bills and buy women unsuitable gifts. If I ever had to make a desert island choice between a guitar and a piano, it would be a very tough call. But the piano would possibly win.

Apart from being a great instrument, a piano is a lovely piece of furniture. A piano, like a cat, will grace a room. As a song-writing tool it is the equal at least of a guitar. A piano is also a bloody liability to move around from home to home. I have moved mine, with much help, at least nine times. If I ever have to sell my current home, which is above a former pub archway, the house will come free but with an extremely expensive piano. By the way, it's now possible to buy upright pianos for small homes. They do make them. Or you could try getting hold of a 3/4-size parlour piano, or even what they used to call a 'ship's piano'. Electric pianos with weighted keys are sort of okay. But, ah... a real piano in your house? No contest, chief.

LESSON 13
LOOK AFTER YOUR IVORIES

If you have a piano, get it tuned at least once a year. And play the thing. They like being played and my own theory is that they stay in tune a bit longer if they're played and loved. One thing I used to do in my ignorant young days was to put drawing pins in each piano hammer, so that the flat head of the drawing pin hits the string instead of the felt head of the hammer. This is a great sound. It's also something, I later learned, that old blues bar-room piano players used to do. Your piano tuner, however, may tell you not to do it. This is because eventually the practice begins to chip the strings, weakening them. The thicker strings can be expensive to replace. But it is a great sound and gives the player a peculiar feeling that the hammers are 'bouncing' off the strings. So, don't do it, alright?

A Steck piano — my second. I've written many non-hits on this

IN BERLIN WITH CHRISTO

For a pop musician with a reasonably futuristic outlook I rarely extend my open-mindedness to developments in the visual arts. I have difficulties with certain art installations, for instance. But I do make exceptions. When I heard a while ago of the death of the Bulgarian artist known as Christo, I was reminded of just such an exception.

Christo Javacheff and his French wife Jeanne-Claude's speciality involved wrapping unusual objects in fabric. Most famously, in 1995, Christo wrapped Berlin's Reichstag entirely in an aluminium-based silver cloth. I visited Berlin shortly after the project was completed. The artist had been forced to negotiate with the authorities for 24 years in order to arrange this installation. Why? No idea. I was only there to play a few gigs and promote an album.

With the Berlin Wall only having come down five years earlier, the newly reunified Germany was still something of a work in progress. The band observed, as we drove into the city centre, that Berlin had been well postered for the concert we were due to play. We were up against stiff competition. Simple Minds, Blondie and Rod Stewart were also in town to play gigs that evening. Luckily, we were only playing a 600-capacity venue, a castle called *Die Insel* situated on a small island in the River Spree. Good as we may have been, we hardly expected to dent the other artistes' ticket sales.

The previous night we'd played a venue just outside Dresden. Typically for the wild former East then, the promoters had skimmed our fee. We, however, needed some money for food while we waited to be paid for the next gig. The international arts world can be fun like that. Once we'd arrived at our Berlin billet, therefore, I suggested that we grabbed a couple of guitars, some gig posters and went busking outside the Reichstag, which was nearby. At this point it was patiently explained to me by our promoter that Christo had recently wrapped the famous monument in cloth. "Will there be plenty of people around?" I asked. "Of course." was his reply. "Good. Then let's crack on," I barked, like an impatient army captain.

Among Christo's conditions for staging this exhibition were that no concerts should be staged in or around the Reichstag during his event. Did I care? We had a gig to publicise and we needed food. While we were setting up, I did have a glance at the artwork. I thought it looked terrible, like a building which was undergoing extensive cleaning. Frankly, I'd rather have seen the Reichstag. Let's face it. It could never have happened in Colchester. Let Christo loose on the Town Hall as an arts initiative? Councillor Bob Russell would have gone Radio Rentals and I'd have been right there behind him. So anyway, we played some songs, collected some money, bought some food and beer, and returned to our accommodation.

Now, Berlin in the summer can be quite humid and headachey. My abiding memory of that tour is of our one free night before the concert. After an oppressively hot day, there was a terrific thunderstorm. I was standing out on the balcony watching the lightning bolts illuminate the city. This, I remembered, was the city of Christopher Isherwood's *Goodbye to Berlin* and his heroine Sally Bowles. My young father, too, had been stationed here very shortly after the war. Following the Reichstag's infamous fire in 1933, Hitler had seized power. The Reichstag, which had been badly damaged inside, wasn't actually used as the dictator's headquarters. That dubious honour fell to the Kroll Opera House over the road. It was the Reichstag, however, which had somehow retained its tenebrous associations with the whole era.

Then, half a century on, Newell goes waltzing up, hoping to see the gaff, only to find that some Bulgarian individualist had done it up like a big roll-mop. Classic. How can I forget that evening, though? Berlin! This historic city rocked by tumultuous crashes and violent lightning. I stood outside on the balcony smoking a cigarette, feeling thoroughly windswept, Wagnerian and epic. I was joined by our drummer, Joe Whitehead. Lost for words, I said "Wow, this is like..." Taking in the *sturm und drang* of it all for a moment, Joe replied in a clipped, military voice. "Yes. Like the old days." That was very wrong. And very funny.

The tour, all things considered, was dodgy. It was badly managed, with daily money worries, my voice on the blink, not enough sleep and a permanent low-level hangover – as was usual. After Berlin we still had Hamburg and

Potsdam to play before going home. Potsdam was good. We saw Frederick the Great's palace, Sanssouci. Oh, and that evening, while returning to the accommodation in the tour bus, I swung a half-hearted punch at the tour promoter, because he'd been such an annoying git. Unluckily, the blow barely made contact, because the wagon happened to lurch, causing me to tumble sideways. Standard tour shenanigans. By then, aged 42, I'd just about had enough of rock gigs. As John Cooper Clarke has often reminded me, "It's not a man's job, is it, Maart?" Looking back, now, I think that at times, it came quite close.

LESSON 14
GO BUSKING

Musicians and singers should, if possible, at some point during their excellent adventure, acquaint themselves with busking. Busking is the closest you will ever come to a straight contract between audience and musician:

1. You play something
2. If they like it, they throw money.

When busking you should, ideally, know at least ten popular songs that nearly everybody passing you might know. Your appearance while performing should be exotic/slightly different. You should perform cheerfully and with enthusiasm, almost as if you're on a big stage somewhere – which in a way you are. It's called The World. You should not seem apologetic or sheepish about your occupation.

Learning songs made popular by other people is a very good and educational thing to do. It will enrich you as a musician and build your confidence. It will also keep you 'match fit' in times of few gigs. It will keep your voice honed for recording. If you can play on the street with confidence, you can play nearly anywhere. And if you earn some money, at least you won't starve.

Nel and I busking at Queensway
 Tube in that London — Oct 1989.
He joined New Model Army —
 I became Martin½ Newell

GIVING VOICE

This is most of what I know about singing and voice care. Firstly, my late mum, who in her time had done a bit of singing, only gave me two bits of advice on the subject.

1. "Never eat nuts before singing." I'd often wondered why this was. One day in the 1970s I found out. While onstage singing one of those big epic rock numbers, I took a deep breath before going for the big note. At this point a small chunk of nut, which must have been skulking in a dental crevice, dislodged itself and went hurtling at warp speed towards the back of my throat. My windpipe caught it and the intended epic note was comprehensively torpedoed, along with my dignity. As I clutched at my throat, a huge involuntary cough sent the trapped nut fragment shooting out of my mouth, into the lights, until, I'd guess, having lost its trajectory, it dropped somewhere into the audience.

2. "Work light." By this, I don't think my mother meant to sing with absolutely nothing inside you, so that you feel weak or slightly light-headed. She meant don't go singing if you've just eaten a big meal. Stage nerves will usually banish hunger pangs anyway and it's not

much good eating when you're all hyped-up. I have found, however, that you'll generally sing or perform better if you're not stuffed. This especially applies to the recording studio. A light Italian meal with a salad will usually get you through a session. Even if it's only minestrone soup, a roll and a cappuccino. But have something, at least.

As you'll surmise from elsewhere in these pages, when I'm recording I regard the song as God. The instruments are merely its handmaidens and the voice its emissary. So, let's start looking at the difficulties of getting that vocal down.

One of my abiding inhibitions, whenever I'm recording a vocal, is that someone in a nearby room, or passing by in the street, will hear my impassioned voice in its isolation, with no enhancements, when I'm sounding like a lone lunatic raving from a padded cell.

Unfortunately, unless you have a totally soundproofed room, or live in a wilderness cabin, you'll just have to deal with this problem. A worse problem is the one of having too much of the outside world getting in and onto your recording. The only crumb of comfort I can offer is that once you've been singing for a while, you may become more obsessed with getting the vocal right than worrying about what the people who hear your muffled vocal dramas will think.

Your voice will sound a lot better if you've had a good night's sleep. Your voice will be better without much more than a smidgeon of alcohol the night before. You should also stay away from any of the other well-known reality-dissolving compounds. But you already know this, don't you? Singing coaches may give you warm-up exercises to do and they work. Professional singers tend not to talk too much during gaps between sessions. There are throat lozenges, pastilles and all manner of other aids. But I find that sleep and no drinking before recording sessions are best.

There's one other thing. I belong to a small group of musicians who meet in a pub once a week. Here we spend two or three hours belting out old pop songs, often in rough harmony. One or two of us do drink a bit of beer, but only enough to keep our whistles wet. I usually come home from these sessions with aching fingers and a slightly worn voice. But here's the useful thing: if I have a vocal to do on a recording the next day, my voice usually sounds just right. It sounds 'broken in' – slightly husky and cracked at the edges. And it works very well on the recordings. Provided, of course, that I've had a good night's sleep.

Nowadays, even though I'm man of cherishable years, I'm sometimes complimented upon still having a reasonably youthful-sounding voice. I came to a theory as to why it may be true. For six years, pretty much without a break, between the ages of 20 and almost 27, I sang in working rock bands, playing mainly in pubs, clubs and (usually) not very well-appointed venues. Here, the bands for whom I sang would play two 45-minute sets, or longer. In one club where we had a residency, we might play four 45-minute sets on two consecutive weekend nights. We'd start at 9pm and often not finish until just before 2am.

This was my personal Hamburg. Except it was actually another port called Ipswich. During these years, which took up much of the 1970s, my voice which began as an immature post-teenage voice, was strengthened, made more confident and hardened up a little.

Then I became chiefly a recording entity, a 'studio rat' as some call it. This was possibly a good thing for my voice. Because as I got into my 30s I didn't encounter what I call a 'crisis of authenticity' which some musicians do. They get past 30 and think that, having passed the first flush of youth, they should put away childish things and choose a genre of music with more credibility or gravitas. Having reached this conclusion, like donning less flamboyant clothing, they may explore folk music, jazz, Americana or reggae. Sometimes, having reached a certain level of proficiency, they might join a tribute band. Tribute bands are the musical equivalent of Japanese knotweed. Sure, they'll make good ground cover for a place which is a cultural bombsite, but once they become established, they'll spread out and pretty much nothing else will be able to grow there.

Mainly, though, the ageing pop musician will gravitate towards blues, rhythm'n'blues or sometimes soul music. These forms are all good, they accommodate various levels of virtuosity, and for some they'll provide almost a homecoming of sorts. However, when it comes to the singing of such songs, many singers will make one mistake. In order to prove that they are being true to the music, they attempt to inject a grit into their voice, which in many cases simply isn't there. There's many a time I've sat in a pub garden watching somebody from a perfectly good, middle-class British home, trying to sound like they've just served a ten-stretch on a Louisiana chaingang for armed robbery. Furthermore, they might try to convey that they've been drinking strong liquor and consorting with bad women in a House of Blue Light – whatever that is.

Although the truth of the matter may be that they teach science in a mid-Essex college during the week, this may not be the type of authenticity to which they aspire. Unfortunately – and I hate to piss on the chips here – if you spend your weekend nights in a British pub, belting out swampy blues songs in what you hope might approximate an authentically dirty swamp-growl, then you may well permanently wreck your voice for any other purposes.

I have seen and heard middle-aged Englishmen playing and singing in pub gardens and car parks, trying to be all manner of American heroes. The abiding British affection for 'Americana' looks set to last. Who am I to criticise it? It is music, it is popular, and nobody is made homeless or goes hungry because of people doing it. I once heard a fellow doing a fairly embarrassing approximation of Tom Waits. I don't know if even Tom Waits sounds that gruff. But there's a genuine pathos involved when someone deliberately damages their vocal chords in a doomed bid for Americana authenticity. I began to wonder whether groups of middle-aged Americans ever hold 'Englishama' festivals – singing parochial songs about trains and vanished corner shops, in nasal-sounding three-part harmonies. I came to the conclusion that mostly they probably don't. But how much do I really know?

LESSON 15
YOU'VE GOT MORE THAN ONE VOICE

Do experiment with your voice and how you record it. You may think that you have one voice. But you may also have another voice which you haven't yet discovered. It may be hidden lower down in the vocal register. If your 'other' voice is quiet and won't take pushing too hard, you might need to close-mic it. If, once you've recorded your voice, it doesn't sound very strong, then double-track it. By that, I mean go onto another track and get as close to doubling what you did the first time. On the second run at it, don't sound the tees or other hard consonants at the ends of lines as strongly. Listen to the two vocal tracks together. Are they close enough to each other? Okay, now play back your second track a little quieter than the first one, so that rather than sounding like two of you singing, it sounds more like just one strong voice. Put your lead vocal at 12 o'clock in the stereo and your second voice at about 5 o'clock. Try putting lots of reverb on the second voice, but hardly any on the first voice. Mess about with these concepts for a while. Because you might find something that you like. Well? That's all for now. You want me to give away all my little cheap tricks in one shot?

WHY DIY?

On the morning of my writing this, I've just learned that one of my songs is heading towards 10 million streams on the Spotify platform. The song 'Only a Shadow' was made in the early winter of 1982. It was 'released' if we may call it that, as a DIY cassette album in the spring of 1983. A badly paid part-time kitchen porter at this time, I probably ordered no more than 50 copies from Selecta Sound, our trusty tape-duplication firm. I then got my partner to design a cover. We made photostats of the design, cut them out with kitchen scissors, coloured them in by hand using felt-tip pens and sent a few 'review' copies out to fanzines.

In the pre-internet days, fanzines were the DIY fraternity's main print medium. There was a period in the early 1980s where mainstream music mags like *NME*, *Melody Maker* and *Sounds* ran small review sections for cassettes. They stopped round about mid-1983, as I recall. DIY cassette albums were sufficiently close to the embers of punk rock, that – I'm guessing here – editors kept an eye on us because they didn't want to miss the next revolution.

Mostly, however, the DIY cassette movement quickly became a forum for (ahem) the avant-garde, electro-experimentalists, missed-the-bus hardcore punks and un-signable amateurs. As one example of the now-accredited originators, if not godfathers of DIY music, the

Cleaners from Venus probably did stand out. We were trying to make genuinely good little pop albums, in order to sell them ourselves without the involvement of the wider music industry.

In short, my ambition was to somehow make a "*Revolver* in a garden shed". How did the world react to this notion? Well, mostly, the world didn't come to learn of this notion. But in the small areas of direct contact with those parts of the world then available to me, I was pretty much laughed out of town. To say that people just didn't get it would be self-aggrandising. People didn't care. They weren't interested. My cohorts and I had set sail upon the wide and choppy music-biz ocean using a small homemade log raft, with a pair of tattered underpants for a flag.

Our average cassette sales for any one album over a period of many months was probably not much than a hundred. Our first album, *Blow Away Your Troubles* (1981) wasn't even recorded on a 4-track Tascam Portastudio but on a Sony TC630 reel-to-reel, sound-on-sound tape machine. All the tracks were in 'marvy mono' we boasted. Our next creation, the first to use a 4-track Portastudio, came out a year later. *On Any Normal Monday* was actually reviewed later that spring in *Melody Maker's* cassette section. The review was by the now well-known music writer Patrick Humphries. It was a good review and took up far more column inches than we'd dreamed possible. Its positivity did one major thing – it re-booted my confidence. Someone had finally 'got it'. I wasn't completely bonkers, after all.

That summer, however, my bandmate and co-conspirator, Lawrence 'Lol' Elliott, left Essex to live in

Bath with his girlfriend. The Cleaners from Venus now consisted of me, a few drum tracks which Lol had recorded for me, and a tiny little Sound Master beatbox that I'd bought earlier because of Lol's increasing absences, prior to his leaving for good. Rather forlornly I began making new songs and half-heartedly experimenting with the drum machine. Among those drum tracks which Lol had left me was the one which became 'Only a Shadow'. I'd obviously played a guide bass part while I recorded him. It was a moronic eight-to-the-bar *du-du-du-du-du-du-du-du*.

It was also typical of the way we started our songs in those early years. At some point later on, I must have returned to the song and thought, "Hmm, this is actually pretty good. It sounds crude and primitive, and it should annoy music snobs for its lack of general craftmanship." So I fashioned a nice jangly riff for it – which came out really well. Then I'd have double-tracked it before I beefed up the bridges and the choruses by overdubbing a second guitar. I probably went out to the pub after that.

A day or so later, I'd have devised some sort of melody, scrawled out the lyrics, and hollered them onto the existing track. It's worth mentioning that, round about this time, I'd been helping Ms Celia Hirst, a local jazz-blues singer, to record her demos. I called in the favour and asked her if she could sing a few back-ups for me on the 'Only a Shadow' choruses. While doing this I bunged an unnecessary amount of cheap echo onto the vocal with my trusty WEM Copicat. It's the kind of guy I am. I just don't care, I don't.

Bear in mind that since I was working with a Tascam

4-track, with the bass and drums down across tracks one and two, I only had tracks three and four in which to add the three guitars and four vocals (including Celia's additions). It was a tight squeeze and I had to do a lot of dropping in and out. Despite this, the track sounds remarkably spacious. As I said earlier, it's had almost 10 million listens on Spotify alone. Apart from being a good track, it also remains a big 'fuck off' to the many music industry people who ignored it at the time and 'couldn't hear a single'. Much covered by other bands including MGMT and White Reaper, there have been a few enquiries from the industry about buying the track and maybe giving it a 'proper release'. The answer from me naturally remains, "Fuck off, deaf-lugs, you can't afford me."

LESSON 16
LEAVE SOME BREATHING SPACE

Learn when to leave a track alone. You need space in a recording. Never mind if it sounds a little unfinished or unprofessional. Does it sound beefy and defiant? Does it have some unfilled spaces? Are the spaces really needing to be filled or are they a necessary feature of the track?

Go and listen to Johnny Kidd and the Pirates 'Shaking All Over'. Go and hear Cliff Richard's 'Move It'. These songs are two of the first original British rock'n'roll classics. Both songs are accorded this credit either side of the Atlantic Ocean. And, of course, both tracks feature a lot of breathing space, as does my own 'Only a Shadow'.

Space, as any estate agent will tell you, is a luxury. There are many record producers and musicians who need to re-familiarise themselves with this fact. Go thou and do likewise. As you were, ladies.

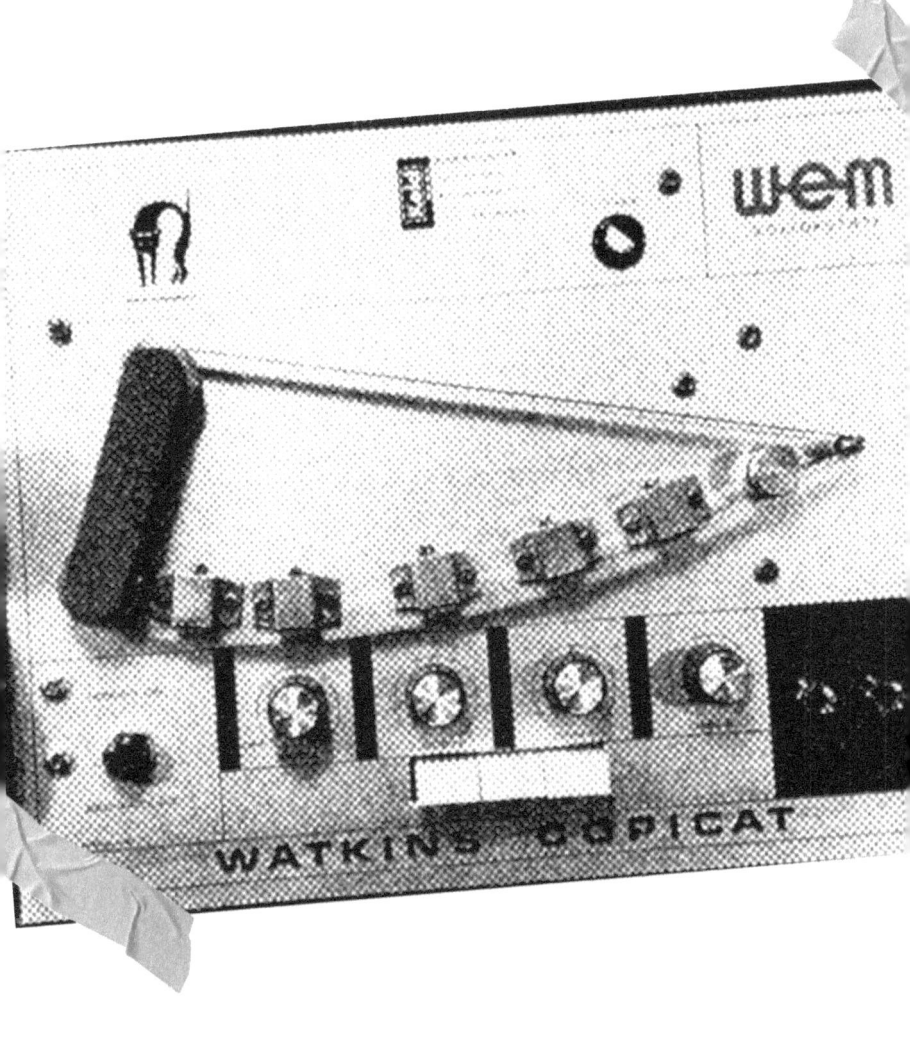

A WEM COPICAT — they cost a fortune now!

SONGWRITING FOR DUMMIES

Ever wondered why so many modern pop songs seem to lack substance or variety these days? Is it, perhaps, because you're an old git, no longer conversant with the idea that each generation must dance to its own drum? Perhaps not. I've been examining a few music-trade podcasts and internet tutorials lately. Popular subjects include: a) How internet streaming trends are affecting songwriting; and b) How to make your songs hold the short attention span of the modern listener.

For some years, I've made a proportion of my income from the songs I've written. Increasingly, this includes revenue from internet streaming rather than from terrestrial sales. I've never had a big chart hit but a handful of my songs have still brought in some money. I've also had songs covered by international acts including MGMT, Alphaville, the Damned and White Reaper. You may not have heard of these artists but in certain parts of the world they're flying.

I began writing songs when I was 14 years old and, more than 50 years later, I'm still doing it. Underneath all the rock ramalama, however, I remain an old-fashioned Tin Pan Alley sort of guy. I grew up in the 1960s, absorbing all the songwriting riches that were then available. I was also influenced by my mum's collection of musicals, along with my dad's liking for Flanders & Swann and other such musical comedy acts. It was a great subliminal schooling. In the 1970s I joined pop groups, where I just about passed muster as a singer and sometimes, rhythm guitarist. Hanging around the music world, however, can be rather like being on a building site. You soon pick up a few relevant skills.

By my mid-20s I could play several other instruments (indifferently) and had learned something of stagecraft and record production. But what I could do really well, it transpired, was writing songs. Somehow, in among the standard pop influences, I'd absorbed bits of Lerner and Loewe, Rodgers and Hammerstein, and several European songwriters whose melodies will be more familiar to people than their actual names. To me these people were songwriting super-beings who, as well as being schooled in music theory and great poetry, were equally deft when deploying humour and whimsy. Pop songwriting has become somewhat impoverished during recent years. The comedown from the mid-20th Century to recent times is comparable to a descent from, say, the Parthenon in Ancient Greece to the wattle and daub dwelling of a Medieval peasant.

Current music industry advice for digital-age songwriters includes, "Stick the chorus at the front of the song, instead of having an intro and a verse." Why? Well, the plan is to reel your attention-span-of-a-goldfish punter in, before they flit elsewhere. Because, if your client doesn't stay for at least 30 seconds, it won't count as a stream and you won't collect your royalties. The imperative, therefore, is for today's songwriter to ditch the subtlety and instead to use the production suite like a medieval trebuchet. It also demonstrates a timeless music-biz contempt for their buyers: minimum output for maximum yield.

This may explain why, when you switch on Your Nation's Favourite Station while bumbling around the kitchen in the morning, you'll suddenly become aware of some full-on sonic assault that compels you to snap the radio off as briskly as you can. The old building blocks of song-writing: intro, verse, bridge, chorus and middle-eights, are no longer required. It's like being told, "Brakes, saddle and handlebars for bicycles? They're just so yesterday!"

So much for the tunes, what about the lyrics? I saved the best for last. Some of this new stuff makes the Archies' 'Sugar Sugar' sound like Gray's 'Elegy'. Common themes include the accusatory "You only want my body at night!" or the mildly threatening, "I'm taking back my love." And who could ignore the resolutely empowered, "I'm on the rampage tonight, Luvvie, so you'd better watch out" – especially if all 15-stone of it is thundering across a hotel lobby towards you dressed in a baby-doll nightie with some kind of carnality on their mind. I'm sure you're familiar – they certainly will be. So, changing the subject, we must ask ourselves whatever happened to heavyweight Sixties lyrics like 'Do Wah Diddy Diddy'?

The facts are that some of us have actually benefited from ignoring the new songwriting guidance, dreamt up, I suspect, by a policy wonk selling spurious workshops sponsored by a streaming platform. Songwriters are not even being told to write to a formula anymore. We're being advised instead to fit a given template. It's so dumb, like telling Mary Berry to make her cakes triangular so that they look good served on a trendy bit of slate. A music publisher, recently, upon hearing some of my stuff for the first time, told me, "Oh wow. You write real songs." He didn't add, "We don't get much call for that sort of thing at our firm," but it was a close-run thing.

It's not all bad news. Streams of my tunes have been more than healthy in recent years. Quick analysis showed that 18-42 year olds are my main demographic. I was mildly surprised. So the art of songwriting's not quite dead yet? Nah. Probably just nipped out to yoga.

LESSON 17
IT'S ABOUT THE SONG, NOT THE BUSINESS

Many of the top songwriters today write in groups of people. Such committees, which are usually assembled by music-biz people, seem to specialise in anodyne concepts. They dwell almost entirely upon normal girl/boy situations. Their pallid efforts will then be sent to an over-production suite – or a 'top recording studio' as they're sometimes called. An appointed vocalist is then recorded, autotuned, bunged through an FX console and then sent home. Nothing happens for ages. In fact, sometimes, nothing happens at all. But if it ever does there will be 'an announce', as the Americans call it. In Brit English, we call this notice of a release date. Actually, records aren't even released these days – they get a 'drop'.

The finished product then 'lands' on the appointed date, with important mainstream deejays, essential TV shows and all points of social media. It's trailed, plugged and played relentlessly until it is dutifully bought by the semi-literate cloth-eared androids who like that kind of thing – I'm sorry, that should have read 'the grateful public'. Many months later the 'song' may be nominated for 'an award of some kind' at a ceremony of the music corporations' own devising. Such events often involve bow ties, monkey suits, glasses of fizz and Martian-looking snacks sent in by an appointed food-designer.

There will be laughter, there will be tears, there will be gown-rending speeches and there will be back-patting. And that's just in the executive toilets a week before the event. A month later nobody can remember what the song sounded like or who won the award. So, the tip here is if you're interested in writing songs of quality that might be remembered for decades, don't get involved with anyone from the music industry. The chances are that you won't meet anyone from the music industry. But if one of them ever does wander into the proceedings because of a security lapse, you can always tell them to fuck off.

THEY READ THE FLYSHIT: RE-EXAMINING CLASSICAL MUSIC

While checking my privilege recently, I became aware of a small spat in the classical music world. The violin virtuoso Nicola Benedetti was responding strongly to a growing perception that classical music is dominated chiefly by white male composers such as Bach, Beethoven and Mozart. Lucy Noble, director at the Royal Albert Hall had stated that while history has left us a legacy of great classical composers, "We must make sure that young people are exposed not just to these white male Titans but to women and those from minority backgrounds." I would normally regard this sort of stuff as yet more fluffing up of feathers in rather posher hen houses than the ones I inhabit.

In the various schools I attended throughout an itinerant childhood, I mostly regarded classical music as the music of the enemy: teachers, headmasters and anyone else in authority. These were the people who'd shouted at me, detained me in chalky rooms, bored me and occasionally hit me. They actually liked this turgid stuff. If it wasn't pop, however, this particular yob wasn't listening. This attitude persisted into my 20s, for it was here that I began noticing the work of film score composers, such as John Barry, Ennio Morricone and Henry Mancini.

Shortly afterwards I also decided that I didn't mind a bit of Baroque. A slippery slope it was, too. Soon came Early music: Marin Marais, then John Dowland, all the way back to Hildegard von Bingen. I retained my dislike of heavy symphonic 19th-Century stodge, however, and opera, which I still can't bear. Yet I became interested in the lives of certain composers. I discovered that just like jazz and rock composers, classical composers frequently had money troubles and suffered poor physical and mental health. They often didn't seem to live very long. Bach died in his mid-60s, Mahler at 51, Beethoven at 56 and Mozart at 35. What I needed to know next was whether or not women and people of colour experienced a rougher time of it than the aforementioned privileged white guys.

In all fairness, I've concluded that they did. For instance, when asked recently, I found that I could only name one female Baroque composer. She was Barbara Strozzi (1610-1677 or thereabouts). A cursory internet search gave me the names of at least a dozen others of whom I'd never heard. Closer study reveals that they're usually either from reasonably wealthy families, or else they're nuns, sometimes both. Why don't we know more of them?

Well, up until a century or so ago, the composing of music, just like the painting of masterpieces and the study of medicine or science, wasn't considered (by the men in charge) a female province. This was not only unfair but downright wasteful. Especially when we consider the sheer amount of talent that must have been either stifled or has remained undiscovered.

With our African-Caribbean composers, however, they get a shockingly bad deal. Scott Joplin is one case in point. An Arkansas railway labourer born around 1867, with the help of his teachers, he developed his own musical knowledge. Predominantly, he pioneered the ragtime piano style that became one of the main portals from classical into jazz music. He then began to publish his own music. He had a publishing 'hit' with the 'Maple Leaf Rag'. Ragtime music went international. It travelled to Europe, influencing the composers Satie, Debussy and several others. Ragtime, however, being by definition 'a craze', died out by about 1920. After that we don't hear much of Scott Joplin until 1970, when the film *The Sting* featured his 1902 rag 'The Entertainer'.

The song's popularity brought Joplin and his other piano rags renewed worldwide fame. This was a mere 53 years after their composer had died in poverty aged 48. Less well-known is that he wrote two operas. His first opera, *A Guest of Honor*, toured briefly. During the course of this tour, however, someone stole the box office returns. The result meant that his 30-strong company payroll and the fees for their lodgings couldn't be found. The opera manuscript and the composer's belongings were confiscated and the opera was lost forever. Joplin's second opera, *Treemonisha*, almost a decade later, was never properly staged because the composer simply didn't have the money. In 1911, after one self-financed, poorly presented and indifferently received preview, *Treemonisha* was forgotten. Joplin, now exhausted and demoralised, suffered a breakdown. He died of neurosyphilis in 1917 and his opera was believed lost.

Then, in 1970, with the revival of interest in his work, a copy was rediscovered. It was staged twice by the Houston Grand Opera, first in Washington in 1972, then on Broadway in 1975, to huge acclaim. Having located a recording on a music site, I listened to it twice through. Despite my avowed dislike of opera, I found Joplin's *Treemonisha* very moving. Diverse in its stylings, it sounds as American in its way as *West Side Story*. Nearly seven decades after he'd built this musical edifice, the establishment finally gave the composer his due. In 1977 he was awarded a posthumous Pulitzer prize. As I said at the beginning of this chapter, I was checking my privilege recently.

LESSON 18
YOU DON'T NEED TO READ MUSIC

A thing that I've noticed about people who've been classically trained in music, say, on piano, cello or flute, is that often – though not always – without their sheet music they can be pretty much useless. Then, often, when they are asked to join in with us feral rock yobs, their playing is frequently stiff, inhibited and suffering from lack of fluidity. It was only then that I began to realise why sheet music had come about. There's nothing clever about it. It's complex, of course, like so many things that have been formulated by trainspotterly men. Never mistake complicated for clever, though. If JS Bach or Handel had owned a little home-recording machine like the ones we use today, do you think they'd ever have bothered ruining their eyesight by candlelight with all those reams of music manuscript?

Less well-known, of course is the fact that both of the composers suffered the most fearful eyesight problems. Does anyone in pop music really need to read music in this day and age? I can only speak for myself. In nearly six decades of playing and writing music, I've rarely wished that I'd learned to read and write music. When asked what I'd do if I needed to score a piece for large string ensemble or a small orchestra, I usually answer that I'd firstly record the bare bones of the piece, before employing someone to annotate it all for me, while I got on with the next job. Life's just too short for that sort of thing.

For not too much money nowadays, you can buy a keyboard called a portable arranger. Roland do one, as do Yamaha. A portable arranger is a keyboard with its own library of ready-made sounds: violins, brass, woodwind, chromatic percussion and all manner of other stuff. Their pre-sets or 'voices' sound a lot more authentic nowadays than they did a few years ago. Such a device will allow the home recordist to experiment. You may ascertain, for instance, whether or not a French horn will work with a harpsichord on your latest masterpiece – or whether it's best to just have a light wash of strings. Conversely, you could choose to simply leave the recording alone. Less may not always be more, but sometimes less will be better.

THE ROLLING STONES IN HYDE PARK

On the 5th of July 1969, just into the last half-year of that mottled decade, the Rolling Stones gave a free concert in London's Hyde Park. Somewhere between a quarter and half a million people attended. I have a photo from the day, with me under a big tree, aged 16 in chalk-stripe hipster bell-bottoms, hippy scarf, green waistcoat, Small Faces haircut, heat headache and nosebleed. It was very hot and at one point I really was beginning to fade unto my own parade. I suffered nosebleeds quite often when I was younger and they used to wipe me out, rather.

Without looking it up, I can remember that the other bands on the bill that day were Screw, whose harmonica-player-vocalist collapsed bleeding, onstage, possibly over-playing with the nerves of it all. There was also Alexis Korner, an early Rolling Stones mentor, now generally regarded as the father of British Blues. Family, one of my favourite bands played, along with the Battered Ornaments and King Crimson – who were stunning. Then, round about mid-afternoon, the Rolling Stones came on and the place went nuts, in a quietly British way.

The Hyde Park concert was originally intended as the debut of the Rolling Stones new boy, Mick Taylor, a 20-year-old blues guitarist previously with John Mayall's Bluesbreakers. He'd replaced the sacked founder member Brian Jones. It's been rumoured however, that Taylor may have been second choice to Rory Gallagher, the Irish guitar wizard.

Gallagher, unfortunately, had had his own foreign tour to do and having run out of time was forced to leave before Keith Richards could be woken up in time to audition him. This at least is the story. Described later by the writer Truman Capote as a "pretty Jean Harlow blonde", Mick Taylor would prove over the next five years to be a sound choice for the band and a formidably good foil for the ragamuffin riffing of Richards.

But the unexpected had happened. Only two days before the concert, Brian Jones was found dead in his swimming pool. For Jones, a young man as notorious as he was famous, it was another first. Hadn't he been the first Rolling Stone? Now he was first of the gang to die and the first member of the 27 Club. Fusty moralists in the national press were keen to claim, too, that Jones' death was beginning of the Permissive Society's chickens coming home to roost. Taylor's intended debut now became his predecessor's funeral wake.

His former bandmates may have put up their bravest cool front when Jones died. Inside, they were shaken to their boots. These were young men, remember, some still only in their mid-20s. They'd already experienced great fame, media condemnation and the spite of a rain-grey British Establishment, even crosser now at having started a generational war that they were beginning to lose. A Rolling Stone death should have been their victory and vindication. That wasn't how our generation saw it.

Now here we all were, in Hyde Park, clapping, shaking our heads, banging Coke cans, idiot-dancing (some of us) or wilting in the heat and trying to keep still (me). The Stones played an undercooked and rather out-of-tune concert for us. Only a curmudgeon would have held it against them, though. If they were rusty, it was because these shell-shocked young guys hadn't played in public for two years. Now they were giving a massive concert, with a new guitarist, only two days after one of their number had died.

So these were the legendary Rolling Stones? They were surrounded by the great and good of the hippy aristocracy, who sat on the stage like so many stoned athelings with their beautiful boho girlfriends. Down the front of the stage, meanwhile, in WW2 German helmets and military surplus caps with chain-trims were the British Hells Angels: the alternative society's newly appointed praetorian guard. Some of them, boyishly slender under the weight of their unexpected responsibilities, looked a little self-conscious. The gig however was peaceful and it must be noted, laced through with a respectful undertone.

Britain in those days was not festival-literate, as it is today. Glastonbury, as an event, hadn't even been invented yet. Most of us didn't quite know how to 'be' at a festival. There was no trouble, however, none that I know about, anyway. The Stones played their raggedy set, thanked us all and then went offstage to huge and affectionate applause. 'Honky Tonk Women', the band's new single, hung around in the pop charts and on the nation's jukeboxes right through to the autumn.

The moddy haircuts, skinny jackets and clean-shaven three-minute pop sensibilities of the mid-Sixties were long gone, replaced now by Zapata moustaches, three-button grandad shirts and hippy scarves. The mood was less frivolous, less fun. Rock had gone 'underground' so the music papers told us. The songs would soon become longer, the concepts more pompous, the flares wider and the hair flappier. When the day was over, I reckon, so was the 'Party after the War' and we all traipsed sadly home to prepare ourselves for the lugubrious and utterly dull early 1970s.

LESSON 19
OUTDOORS IS TROUBLE

The Rolling Stones, much as I love the old darlings, sounded pretty shoddy at the Hyde Park concert. Sure, after a long break from playing live, and the shellshock of one of their number dying only three days earlier, they were sonically a bit tatty.

I really don't like recording outdoors. I love extraneous sounds creeping onto records, but the great outdoors contains rather too many random variables. Of all of these, the wind is the worst. I've played open air gigs, where a stiff breeze has blown the onstage sound sideways, as if it were a sheet on a line. Aeroplanes, lorries and motorbikes will also play their part in the recordist's problems.

During the early to mid-70s, the late hippy period, quite a few people tried recording outside, with varied results. About the best of these was a Chichester band called Heron, who recorded a couple of rather charming folky albums in a garden by the Thames (I think). They wanted to get the crickets and summer birdsong on their recordings and it did actually work – if you liked that sort of thing. Giles Smith and I, as the Cleaners from Venus in 1985 recorded almost the whole of a song called Clara Bow outdoors – and it worked. It was a beautiful, still, early summer morning and we were lucky – we only got a lorry and a few ducks on the tape with us. Most of the time the random variables will drive you bonkers. Almost better to record the birds and insects separately and build yourself a folio to dub onto your recording later. Or buy an album of BBC sound effects – because they do tend to be really well recorded. As a rule, I'd say by all means try recording outdoors. But do take pop-filters for the microphones and don't expect it will turn out as you hoped.

MEANWHILE... IN ABBEY ROAD

The control room of Studio One at Abbey Road is, to use a cliché, something like the flight deck of a starship. To get there, you go up those famous front steps, check in at the desk, proceed down the corridor, through various doors, until eventually, Studio One appears in front of you. It's nothing like my home-recording set-up. It's the difference between a Medieval peasant's dwelling, and a penthouse flat in Mayfair. I just wanted to let you know that I have actually been in some good studios and I do know, roughly, how they work. I'd like to keep it clear that recording-wise, I'm a wattle and daub, sedge-woven hovel kind of guy. It's just that I think that sometimes it's good to know what the enemy's got. Okay?

Abbey's Road Studio One is actually a sound-factory bolted onto the back of a Georgian townhouse, one which way back was reportedly a brothel. The control room looks out onto a great warehouse space large enough to accommodate two orchestras, or possibly four or five Spitfires. Here in November 1931, Abbey Road's first recording session took place. 'Land of Hope and Glory', played by the LSO and conducted by Sir

Edward Elgar. Among those present was Elgar's bezzie mate, George Bernard Shaw.

It was here too, in the spring of 1967, that a 40-piece orchestra and a number of pianos were used by Paul McCartney to create that final apocalyptic chord which closes the *Sgt Pepper* album.

Lastly, it was here, in early 2005, that I sat in the control room, observing a 65-piece orchestra overdubbing strings onto a song I'd written three years earlier. Listening to my work now oozing from the speakers, vastly transformed by an opulent cushion of strings, I quite forgot myself and blurted out. "I wrote that!" The producer remarked dryly, "Yes, we know, Martin. That's why you're here." The recording engineers laughed. I said, "I'm sorry. It's just that... well, I'm not used to hearing myself being done by an orchestra." More laughter. I shut up and sank further into my seat behind the mixing desk.

The song finished and the conductor's voice twanged from the monitor. "D'you wanna come through and meet the orchestra, Martin?" I was directed to a door leading out into the cavernous auditorium. A seeming half mile away I saw the orchestra as I padded like a wary cat towards the rostrum. "Ladies and gentlemen," said the conductor, "This is Martin Newell, whose songs we have been working on."

The ladies and gentlemen put down their bows and instruments and applauded me. I was moved. At first, I thought that I might cry but instead a croaky little voice that didn't feel like mine said simply, "Thank you."

A classics bore later informed me, rather loftily, that it was standard etiquette when orchestra players meet the composer. They have to applaud you or something. As I'm still essentially an Essex yob, however, I replied, "Happened to you a lot, has it, Chief?"

I first met Richard Shelton, singer and actor, in 2002, at the BBC, when he was playing the part of Frank Sinatra in a west-end play *Rat Pack Confidential*. He'd just delivered a hypnotic rendition of 'In the Wee Small Hours' live on BBC national radio. Why, I asked him afterwards, did he think so many jazz and show singers still sang the Great American Songbook, often to the exclusion of almost all else? Richard replied very simply: "Because nobody nowadays writes songs that good." I told him that I was trying to do it. Someone has to, don't they? I led him into an unoccupied studio next door, sat down at a piano and played him a song, 'Grenadine and Blue.' He asked me who wrote it. "I did," I said. "For Tony Bennett... I sent it to his son."

Tony Bennett, I later learned, has two sons. One looks after his music, the other looks after his art business. Tony was also a talented artist. Unfortunately, I'd sent the song to the wrong son. When I learned this, I lost heart and gave up. "Anyway," I said brightly, "it's a new song. Nobody's done it yet. And I can't do it myself, because it really needs a proper singer. Like you. Would you like it?"

Time passed. Then one day Richard announced to me that he was going into Abbey Road with an orchestra to make a whole album and did I have any other songs? I got cracking. They eventually selected five of my compositions. As a closet Tin Pan Alley hack, I now felt truly outed. There I'd been, all those years, imagining that I was a Pete Townshend or a Ray Davies, when all along I'd really been a cheap Rodgers and Hammerstein wannabe.

Right out of the blue, Richard got this big part in the UK's other favourite rural soap, *Emmerdale*, as Dr Adam Forsythe. I knew it would come to no good. He ended up murdering someone and then committing suicide while in prison. His character, I mean, not Richard. But his album? It fared… okay, you know? But maybe not as well as it might have done if Richard hadn't been busy being a full-time soap star. It came to a point, in fact, where my then ten-year-old daughter would gesture at the TV and say. "Ooh look, it's Richard again."

After his character's suicide, everything went quiet. Then, a few years later, Richard casually informed me that he'd moved to Los Angeles and was making an album in Capitol Records Studio B with some of Sinatra's old sidemen. They'd scored one of my songs for strings and it was destined for the new album. "Wow", I said.

A while later I returned home in a daze after seeing Richard, with the Denmark Street Big Band playing a lunchtime concert in Dean Street, Soho, while promoting the new album. They were playing my song again. And all because years earlier I'd posted a demo to the wrong Tony Bennett son. Songwriting. Funny old game, innit?

LESSON 20
STATE-OF-THE-ART STUDIOS ALSO BREED TURKEYS

Very famous, state-of-the-art studios are great. The engineers and producers who work there regularly will often be the best in the business. When you stand in a top recording studio for the first time, listening to the play back ("Now let's hear what it sounds like on the Big Ones") you may be suitably awestruck. And rightly so.

Just remember, though, that large expensive studios, as well as being the home of immortal works of art, are responsible for an awful lot sonic landfill too. Beautifully recorded turkeys made by very wealthy and badly advised burnouts will often emerge from such opulent workstations. The saying that 'you can't polish a turd' is true. So is the follow-up saying: "But you can roll it in glitter." Unfortunately neither of these hypothetical acts will compensate for a lack of good songs.

Luckily, every so often some recorded gem will just as easily emerge from the land of portastudios and eggbox soundproofing. My own long music career and that of Cleaners from Venus is existing proof that not all artistes respond well to being told, "Great songs! Now let's go and record them in a proper studio with a good producer." So much for record companies and music biz movers. If it doesn't feel right, just say "Fuck that shit."*

*Alternatively, you may prefer to contact the company involved with a polite written response, along the lines of, "Unfortunately my colleagues and I are of the opinion that groups of businessmen with record companies are on their way out. As a consequence, we regret to say that your application to ruin our music has not been successful upon this occasion. You wankers."

HOW WE FORGOT TO WRITE SONGS

I learned recently that a US songwriter Ryan Tedder, who's written material for Beyoncé, Ed Sheeran and Taylor Swift among others, claimed that music streaming on Spotify and other digital platforms was being dominated by the Beatles, Queen, Fleetwood Mac and other music mastodons. This, he said, lessened the chances of newer artists being streamed.

The really interesting thing to emerge here, however, was that some 65 per cent of people listening to these golden oldies were not, as we might have expected, reactionary old gits. They were people under the age of 34. How, asks your resident old git, is this unfair? Well, Ryan reckoned that newer tunesmiths don't stand a chance against 50 years of established golden greats.

It's a fair point, but it's obvious to me why younger people might be opting for the old over the new. It's better quality kit, plain and simple. A good song is a good song and the art of writing songs has, in recent decades, declined somewhat. In the early 1960s, newcomers like the Beatles, Brian Wilson, Tony Hatch and Ray Davies had to contend with a seemingly unassailable old guard, comprising Rodgers and Hammerstein, Lerner and Loewe, Cole Porter, George Gershwin, Ivor Novello and Noël Coward. Such composers routinely displayed musical brilliance, while their lyricists penned moving and often ingeniously witty words. With the 1960s arrived a new generation, partly inspired by the old masters, yet with new tricks and production values of their own. Unfortunately, at time of writing, our current songwriters, praised as they may be, don't always seem as deft as their predecessors. One reason for this might be an over-reliance on modern recording technology which, although vastly better now than it was 30 years ago, does seem to make for slipshod songwriting.

When I was a 17-year-old wannabe songwriter, along with another older lad who wrote the lyrics, I went down to London to do the rounds of record companies. We didn't even have a demo tape, just some songs and my guitar. At one company, a record producer actually invited us into his office and listened to me while I played our material. He turned me down, of course. I was way too raw. But he also told me that I was on the right track. "If a song is any good," he said, "it will stand up when sung by one voice, accompanied by one instrument. All the production gloss, along with the greatest session players in the world cannot turn a dud into a great song." Best advice I ever had.

The modern expectation of what might qualify as 'a song' has changed somewhat. Today's productions may sometimes consist of a nursery-rhyme chorus chanted repeatedly over a dominant drumbeat. At various intervals, a rapper – often someone with the vocal delivery of a racehorse commentator – will chunter something resembling a list of sociological grievances over the actual song. He may, while he's at it, offer to pop a cap in your bottom. In addition, he might venture that since he undoubtedly has a bigger winkie than yours, your *[insert derogatory word for a woman]* – should you happen to be in a relationship with one – will show no hesitation in deserting you in his favour. 'Windmills of Your Mind' or 'MacArthur Park' this stuff is not. This same creation may nonetheless be deemed 'a banging tune' by some baffled mainstream radio producer ordered to play it, while pedalling frantically to keep a) 'It' real, and b) Their job.

The aptly named 'banger' or 'choon' will then be given rotation airplay on national mainstream radio for a month. The diminishing number of ageing listeners at whom it's aimed, will gasp indignantly at the racket, before pelting across the kitchen to turn it off. The public's steadfast refusal to accept much of the sonic landfill touted by the music industry hardly constitutes a cultural apocalypse. There's no law dictating that we must change our listening habits every few months and anyway, many people just want a bit of aural wallpaper, while they're doing the chores.

Everyone loves a good song. Few, nowadays, know how to write one. It's a waste of time attending songwriting workshops, however. If the people who organised such tenuous gatherings knew how to write immortal songs, believe me, they wouldn't be teaching lesser mortals. They'd be in Switzerland, having breakfast with a recently divorced Italian film star. Or maybe that's just me.

LESSON 21
STUDY THE GREAT SONGWRITERS

So what should a would-be songwriter do? You're asking the right guy. Firstly, develop the principles of a bombsite rat. Go and study, without prejudice or preconceptions: Hollywood musicals, Anglican hymns, the Beatles, Burt Bacharach, Lionel Bart and all the other greats. Then absorb the best rhyming poetry you can find, before plundering everything within earshot. Now post your pillaged creations up on platforms like Spotify, Deezer, Apple etc. Work social media relentlessly. Employ some young digital adept who knows how to tweak algorithms. Give them a fair cut of the dosh. Refuse to compromise and never listen to anyone from the arts world. They know nothing. Be kind to your listeners, especially the younger listeners, because they live their lives and their dreams through great songs. That's why many of them love the Beatles, the Stones, Abba and old musicals. Great songs help people through bereavement, bad times, psychiatric illness and more. Humanity needs great songs. Just don't expect to make a living off them immediately. Off you go then.

DON'T... TAKE IT EASY

A pop concert in Hyde Park 2022. The Eagles, now in their 70s, are playing onstage. Grown men are brawling in the VIP enclosure. Stewards in hi-viz vests are attempting to contain it. Audience members, phones held aloft, are filming it. What's wrong with this picture?

Pop music as most of us know it, stammered into life in the late 1950s. Culturally, therefore, it's still relatively young, although only a few of its original pioneers still survive. Not all pop stars end up dead, deranged, or damaged as a result of mucking about with drink and drugs. Nevertheless, some of them never really grow up. Their fans on the other hand, not always having had either the time or money to continue living in Neverland, are usually forced to grow up, get jobs and do something sensible. By middle age, clad in more sober plumage than in their peacock youth, people who were once dyed-black goths, pink-Mohican punks, mods, rockers, hippies, new romantics or whatever, are in responsible employment. Some end up running hospitals, police stations, colleges, newspapers or even governments.

Whenever I meet such people, they'll sometimes surprise me with their knowledge and abiding passion for long-gone music trends. One former regional newspaper editor whom I spoke to admitted to being a keen Who fan. I enjoy asking people of a certain age which music it was that lit up their young lives. Answers can be fascinating, because mostly it's really hard to guess. I once asked a director of a swish modern art gallery what music she'd liked in her youth. I was expecting David Sylvian, Eno, John Cage, Miles Davis, that sort of thing. She was actually big on Billy Ocean and Duran Duran.

Conversely, former PM David Cameron expressed a fondness for the music of the Smiths. The band's left-leaning guitarist Johnny Marr, upon hearing this news, was so dismayed that he issued a statement saying, "Prime Minister, stop saying that you like the Smiths. I forbid you to like it." Author JK Rowling, incidentally, is also known as a keen Smiths fan.

But who'd have thought that well-loved snooker ace Steve Davis would have been mad about Gentle Giant and the outer reaches of prog rock. He even organised it for the French band Magma to play a UK concert, much to the delight of the band's smallish UK following at that time.

The thing is, that once the effrontery of youth has been stifled by the need to fit in sartorially with one's new adult responsibilities, the outlandish costumes are cast off. Time, too, will visit its own peculiar vandalism upon us, so that many youthful hairstyles are then rendered impossible to resuscitate. Underneath it all, though, our passions still smoulder. A few years ago, in a Zoom conversation with my old songwriting partner Captain Sensible, he told me that his band the Damned were going out on tour again. I asked, "D'you still get all those beefy middle-aged guys with spiky leather jackets and pink Mohicans, pogo-ing down the front?" The Captain looked at me and said candidly, "When we go out onstage these days, it's like looking out over a sea of boiled eggs."

Back in 'the now' – as sports commentators like to say – I found it hard to believe that the Eagles, those mega-famous West Coast hippies, had unwontedly found themselves providing the soundtrack for an outdoor punch-up. Formed over half a century ago, the Eagles played the sort of deluxe country rock music which during the 1970s was popular in the flappy denim and cheesecloth camp. Being more of an Alex Harvey/Dr Feelgood fan back then, I wasn't mad about such stuff. But fair play to them, it was easy listening and highly radio-friendly. The gurgling gentlemen farmers who manned Radio One's turbid turntables for most of the 70s played the Eagles' records ad nauseam. Despite it all, I did feel mildly sorry for the band when fighting broke out in sight of the stage, in the 'VIP enclosure'. The Eagles had a VIP enclosure? This was not a backstage area for actual celebs, you understand. This was more like a corporate experience involving hotels, marquees, a cloakroom, fizz, food and rather posher loos.

The prices for your 'diamond VIP experience'? A foodbank-friendly £400 was one offer that I found. You think Glastonbury doesn't allow this sort of thing? Think on, flower-child. If you have that kind of cash, you too can now avail yourself of a corporate-style pint and punch-up almost anywhere. How alternative. But it's something which has its ancestry in 19th-Century racecourse meetings. In fact, I think they still do provide drink-fuelled mass brawls at Royal Ascot, don't they? So we're in fine British tradition. And the song that the Eagles were playing during the hostilities? It was 'Take it Easy'. Yes, I thought you'd like that.

One question that American friends ask is: "Why do you English people speak in your own accent and yet sing in an American one?" This is a very good question. I have strong childhood memories of my mum, singing in the kitchen while she was doing the dishes. A keen amateur singer, from the late 1940s onwards she liked a lot of American crooners and Broadway musicals. She had the most crisply English of speaking voices and yet, when singing, she rolled her Rs in imitation of the many US crooners whom she heard.

Until the Beatles came along in 1963, there persisted an idea among many pop fans that only the Americans could write proper pop songs. This was especially true in the wake of Elvis Presley and rock'n'roll music in general. A lot of such stuff would have sounded embarrassing in any kind of English accent, let alone British newsreader-English or RP as it is sometimes known. During the 1950s and early 1960s it began to seem as if an English accent was now only acceptable when singing our own native comic songs.

Even today, there's a substantial number of British people between, say, 40 and 70 years old who are adherents of that music known as 'Americana'. Americana is a hotchpotch of alt-country, Appalachian bluegrass, swampy blues and dustbowl-era laments.

At the time of writing, Americana festivals are very popular in the UK. Grown men and women from perfectly good English middle-class homes will happily don check shirts, dungarees, silly fringed waistcoats, baseball caps and similar prêt-à-porter items in order to be seen at such events.

Americana is considered gritty, authentic and life-affirming. It goes with barbecue-style cuisine (or 'cookouts') and hog roasts conducted in pub car parks. A proportion of British musicians have now adopted the Americana clothing style, while singing America-themed lyrics in suitably theatrical American accents. Sometimes they buy guitars which resemble kitchen colanders. A proportion of their public may fail to understand quite why. But on balance it may possibly seem more authentic when observed wholesale.

Back to the Eagles. The Eagles, Californian country-rock superstars of the 1970s onwards, exemplified early commercial Americana. Hugely popular with many late-wave hippies throughout the 1970s, the Eagles ruled both the music charts and airwaves. This was all perfectly legitimate, of course. They were after all, Americans. What didn't ring quite true were their many pallid British imitators and the daft UK record company wonks, who considered this situation acceptable. Some of us didn't agree.

To people such as myself, British country rock sounded anything but authentic. It was unoriginal, fake and embarrassingly bland. As Captain Sensible once snarled while the Eagles song 'Lying Eyes' was playing on the radio: "File under 'Reasons Why Punk Was Invented'."

Here we were, in the depressed mid-1970s in council-estate England with its uncollected rubbish and greyscale skies. And yet, there were these grinning, be-flared latter-day British hippies listening to the Eagles, smoking Marlboros, sipping Jack Daniels and pretending for all the world that it was Laurel Canyon. What the actual?

LESSON 22
DON'T PRETEND TO BE FROM SOMEWHERE YOU'RE NOT

One of the reasons I began home recording was so that I could make something more honest and homemade – not necessarily in a punk-rock style but recognisably not Californian. Until almost the 1990s, hip easy listening and laid-back Californian dross were often what the major record companies were still trying to force-feed us. So, the tip here is that you should try to make original recordings that represent and depict your own background – rather than in imitation of something you watched on an American TV programme. Even if your work sounds a bit lo-fi, who cares what the record companies think? They know nothing. Look at the crap they've been trying to sell us all for all these years. We deserve better. It's your job to invent it, okay?

THE SIXTIES

Decades, culturally at least, rarely begin and end when the calendars dictate that they do. The 1960s for instance, for me, probably started in early 1963 with 'Please Please Me'. It ended in mid-1969 with 'Honky Tonk Women'. Fifty years later, I marvel at how the time shimmied by at such a clip. I was barely seven when the Sixties dawned. Even then, it wasn't until the Beatles showed up that things seemed to really get going.

There'd been signs, of course. Two pop musicals *The Young Ones* (1961) and *Summer Holiday* (1962) had successfully filled the country's cinemas. Seen nowadays, even if they seem corny, both still brim with youthful exuberance. They show the optimism of a country happily hauling itself out of post-war austerity. Starring Cliff and the Shadows they depict boisterous young Brits, all in gainful employment and, for a change, not dressed like their dads.

In *Summer Holiday*, presciently, the film begins in monochrome before quickly turning to colour. A recap of the plot: four young mechanics refurbish a London bus and take it to Europe for a holiday, with a view to setting up a business. It was radical in its way. Two decades earlier, the only reason a group of young Brits might leave Britain would be, say, to help recapture a continent recently invaded by someone who'd got a bit above himself.

On both sides of the Atlantic, when the Sixties finally arrived, it swanned in with a curvy new escort on its arm – optimism. The Space Age was upon us. Now came the soundtrack. It's sometimes been said of the new era that it felt 'as if almost anything was possible'. For a pop-crazed English boy like me this was certainly true. Yet there was something more esoteric blended in with that optimism. It was a yearning for some indefinable thing, a gypsy caravan recently passed by but still worth running after. Being too young for the party, however, which I then was, was perfectly as useless as being too old for it. I remember watching the film *Breakfast at Tiffany's* on TV when I was about 12 and wishing that I could somehow escape into this romantic world. I didn't even know where to start.

Even as the 1960s unfolded, with fantastic new pop records now being released on a weekly basis, I had the uneasy feeling that it was all going too fast to last. I wondered, as I entered my teen years, whether there'd be any pop groups left for me to join. Or whether there'd be a Julie Christie or a Patti Boyd still waiting for me when I finally came of age. Pop music by now was impossibly good. In 1967, June's pop charts alone could boast 'Waterloo Sunset', 'A Whiter Shade of Pale', 'Pictures of Lily' and Jimi Hendrix's 'The Wind Cries Mary' – all in one Top 10 listing. Armed with this evidence, therefore, I'd just like to tell this court that I don't merely think that pop music was better 50 years ago. I bloody well know it was. 1967 was surely the peak of it. Never again would pop seem so diverse, so inventive and so perfectly crafted as it did that summer.

Within a year, however, the party was flagging, joints had been dogged-out in the cake and psychedelia had gone stale. In July 1968, as the Beatles began to drift apart, they closed their Apple Boutique, allowing an eager public to swarm into their Baker Street premises to an undignified scrimmage over unsold stock, now free-of-charge. In the US weeks earlier, Bobby Kennedy had, like his older brother John, died from an assassin's bullet.

Swinging London became a cynical, more commercialised version of its earlier self. The smarter mods had grown their hair and become hippies. Their disillusioned baffled younger brothers had shaved theirs off to become skinheads. The Rolling Stones at this time seemed constantly in trouble with the law.

By the January of 1969, when your 15-year-old correspondent began work in an office in Farringdon Street, a chillier wind was hacking along the London pavements. One spring evening, with my Rolling Stone haircut and my little Carnaby Street military jacket and bell-bottoms, I was punched unconscious, given a good kicking and left lying in a London street by some lads who thought I needed to be "taught a lesson". The people where I worked told me, "That's what you'll get if you go around dressed like that." Confused, ill and suffering flashbacks, I walked out of the job.

Then, in early July, Brian Jones, who'd just left the Rolling Stones, was found dead in his swimming pool. It was the first casualty of the era. For me, it was the death of the sunny decade which he'd represented. His unofficial wake was the Rolling Stones free concert in Hyde Park. I was now 16. I was there. It proved not to be the end of the Rolling Stones, but for me it was the end of the 1960s.

LESSON 23
WATCH YOUR POP-STAR STYLE

Beware the winds of fashion. They're great when you're young and can ride them with impunity. But they can be chilly if they suddenly change, as music and clothes fashions do. If you're caught out when the party's over, the world can become a cruel place. A 50-year-old wearing a Punk's Not Dead T-shirt is one tragedy. A 60-year-old New Romantic might be worse. Young hippies once looked beautiful. Old hippies are merely 'old hippies'. Try to develop a style of your own. Perhaps wear a timeless blend of vintage and classic clothes. One of the most successful bands in the world dress like a team of carpet fitters. They're called Coldplay. The Rolling Stones, another highly successful act, with more crag to their collective features than Mount Rushmore, remain somehow a focus of almost universal fascination. If it truly suits you, wear it.

POP FESTIVALS 50 YEARS ON

It's festival time. Never in the field of human congress have so many paid so much for so few basic facilities. Latitude or Glastonbury? (Other festival brands also exist). On balance I preferred Latitude. The newer of the two events, Latitude in Suffolk has always seemed a little gentler. From the outset, it seemed to have learned from other festivals' failings. The necessaria, to wit, their bogs, were never quite as unspeakable as Glasto's. But then I never liked festivals much anyway. I've performed at more of them than I've ever attended as a punter.

From the late 1960s until 2000, music festivals were rather a minority pursuit. Most local councils, for a start, simply wouldn't allow them. Not even for one day. They were synonymous with hippies, noise, drugs and mess. The killjoys had a point. Even in sodden 1997, when I performed at Glastonbury, some of the revellers were suffering trench foot. This occurred because after their trendy ex-German-army combat boots had become soaked, they lined them with plastic shopping bags. Soldiers are trained never to do this. They look after their boots instead.

Other Glastonbury-goers contracted E. coli from wallowing in mud which had only recently been vacated by Mr Eavis's cattle. The perils of festival tummy, terrible toilets, and insomnia caused by campers two tents away jamming on sax and bongos all night, were still in evidence. In 1997, however, the BBC began, very cautiously, patronising Glastonbury. They took the job over from Channel 4, treating it as if it were some kind of Glyndebourne for the scrumpy and dreadlocks set. That's when festivals started their inexorable trudge into the mainstream. Glastonbury began booking headliners, like erm... well, Rolf Harris actually. This was before his fall from grace, proving thereby that postmodern irony can be a slippery slope.

It soon became quite the thing to book mainstream showbiz headliners like Tony Bennett, Tom Jones and stars of similar stature for the main stage. By the nondescript Noughties, some of the posher money realised that they'd been missing out. They badly wanted to see their beloved Coldplay and Radiohead but... Oh but what, Tamara? Well, weren't there all those interminable traffic queues to have to deal with? And, after gaining entry to what was rapidly becoming Greater London in Tents, wasn't there still all that mud and those so-called 'toilets' to contend with?

And so, some entrepreneur, some genius, had an idea: why not set up a corporate hospitality version just next door? First you book a block of tickets. Then, on a site rented from one of Mr Eavis's neighbours, you install some cushy yurts with double-beds and hot showers. Throw in a cocktail bar, some bespoke catering and – shazam! –

you have a top people's Glasto Experience. Having then assembled Henrietta, Araminta, Sebastian, Hugo and all their friends at London's City airport, you chopper them out to their Glampsite. After the Champagne welcome, they board one of the 24-hour shuttles to the festival and sweep through a special picket gate, just in time to catch Lawrence and the Cash Machine. Once they've had an elegant sufficiency of rubbing shoulders with the hoi polloi, they can make their way back to the picket gate, flash their passes, board the shuttle bus and make all the mud and smells go away again. And that, boys and girls, so an embittered old hippy once told me, was how glamping was invented.

After that breakthrough, it was only a matter of time before small, semi-private, word-of-mouth festivals evolved. Some of these you won't have heard of unless you've met someone who's been there, or you've actually been booked to perform at one. Everyone's in on the act now. At one recent local(ish) event, I learned that there'd been a 'VIP area'. An extra 40 quid allowed you into a cordoned-off section to drink fizzy stuff and mingle with selected D-listers from sundry reality TV shows. Heartwarming stuff, eh? I don't think we're in Canvas anymore, Toto.

Glastonbury itself is now so firmly welded into mainstream culture that the BBC will usually arrive before you do, standing at the gate like an overly jolly prefect at the school dance, advising you which acts you should 'rock-out' to. Then they'll edit up the various highlights to use as Polyfilla in their iPlayer schedules. However jaundiced I may sound, though, I can't honestly support the complaint that the middle classes have taken over 'our festivals'. Any sort of cultural enjoyment in a muddy field was a pretty middle-class construct in the first place. No working-class dandy that I ever met in my youth would have risked getting his Chelsea boots and crushed velvet trousers ruined by mud. Not after a week slaving in a ghastly factory in order to be able to afford them. How much nicer to be in a smoky Soho cellar club, speeding on Dexedrine spansules or French Blues under ultraviolet lights and chatting up some chick – perhaps one who was wearing what your mum would have called 'an unsuitable amount of make-up'. Or maybe that was just me. Latitude, however, has one big advantage. If you live within a 40-mile radius of that particular festival, at 9am that Saturday morning, Waitrose will be all but deserted and you can go shopping in peace.

LESSON 24
DON'T BOTHER WITH MUSIC FESTIVALS

I'll say it again: don't even bother with music festivals. They belong to the 20th century – like polio, rickets and world wars. They haven't really been about music for decades. Take advantage of the fact that most of the music twats you know will be either playing there, getting trollied there, or both. You're missing nothing. Instead, save your money, stay home and get down to a nice quiet weekend of home recording.

IN ANDY'S SHED

The picture turned up in a batch of old photos that were being restored for use in a documentary. Taken in 1993 at a record-mastering studio in London's West End. it shows two men in their late 30s, looking absorbed in their work.

In late August of 1993, Andy Partridge of the band XTC and I knew that there'd be a photographer arriving but we really were pressed for time. We'd been putting the finishing touches to what turned out, at that particular time, to be the most important album of my life. Upon its release that autumn, Rolling Stone magazine in the US hailed it as a classic on a par with the Flamin' Groovies Shake Some Action. Even the standardly sniffy British rock press gave it a few grudgingly good reviews. We made the album over a six-month period in Andy's garden shed in Swindon. Andy at this time was a noted, much sought-after record producer. Even while I was working with him, during the course of a few weeks, first Bob Geldof, then Morrissey, then Midge Ure's people telephoned to ask whether Andy would be interested in producing them. Morrissey was not long out of the Smiths at that point, and a big deal.

"Morrissey?" I remember saying. "Wow. Come on Andy, surely you've got to do that." Andy didn't want to.

Andy Partridge was even more awkward, even less of a showbiz schmoozer than I am. You see, what they never tell you when you're in the music industry, is that nobody forces you to attend those parties, avail yourself of the grog, or inhale anything that you don't want to. You can just stay in the studio and get on with your work if you wish. Some of us actually do. It was mostly by chance that I was even working with Andy. In 1993, XTC were a much bigger name than I was. They'd had all these hits: 'Generals and Majors', 'Towers of London', 'Senses Working Overtime', 'Sgt. Rock (Is Going to Help Me)' and the one that nearly everyone remembers, 'Making Plans for Nigel.'

Known for their quirky English style, in early 1986 the band had been paired with the famous US producer, Todd Rundgren. The album which resulted, *Skylarking*, went double-platinum in America. That's 2 million sales. Regarded in the US as one of the best albums of 1980s, here in Britain, *Skylarking* was met by the music press with relative indifference. For a fickle London rock press, XTC, a provincial band, could do no right. They'd stopped touring some years earlier and Andy Partridge had naturally gravitated towards production work.

In 1991, along came Blur, an up-and-coming Essex Indie band. Soon afterwards, they and Andy were put together for what later became Blur's second album *Modern Life is Rubbish*. The pairing hadn't gelled, however, and after four or so songs the project was abandoned. Blur's loss was my gain. My record company were keen for Andy and I to work together. They thought that our shared provincial 'Englishness' might work. They were right. Andy and I hardly stopped laughing and joking from the time we met. I didn't want to work in London or indeed, to return to working in large studios.

I felt that the heart had gone out of music. I wanted to make a "garden-shed *Revolver*". Over the next six months that's precisely what Andy Partridge and I endeavoured to do. There were no rock star shenanigans. We only worked by day. Andy was happy with that too. There used to be a quaint idea among certain musicians that true art only happens if you start work late at night, having 'warmed up' your voice etc etc. I think it comes from reading too many articles and books about famously wasted rock stars. You can try it, of course. But what I used to find was that most people become disoriented, sleepy or drunk, and all the jobs take twice as long and then only have to be done again on later sessions. I'd borrowed a flat in Bath for six months, commuting to Swindon and back each day. I'd turn up at Andy's house every morning about 9.30, then we'd walk his dog in the nearby park before having a cup of tea and starting work.

One day, he mentioned a climbing Japonica quince which had become rather overgrown on the pergola in his garden. He talked about getting someone to prune it. I said, "Oh, I could do that. Have you got some secateurs and some steps? I'll sort it out while you get the drums recorded." I was up the steps when he came out of the shed briefly. "Will you be alright up there, Martin?" I laughed like a drain. Before I ever met him, and perhaps because he'd written songs with titles like 'Love on a

Farmboy's Wages', I'd assumed that he'd done a certain amount of outdoor jobs, as I had done. But he was rather an armchair ruralist, really.

As a record producer, however, he was brilliant – and with the hearing of a bat. He described his production style as "Somewhere between Mussolini and Santa Claus". If he heard me sing anything even slightly suspect, he'd make me re-do the part over and over again. But if I ever I began to fray around the edges, he'd stop me. "D'you wanna cup of tea?" he'd ask. Andy was actually very kindly. And the album? It was called *The Greatest Living Englishman*. It's rarely been out of stock.

It was the album that all the music-biz people who thought I had 'potential' wanted me to make. A record with 'more conventional production values', has been a common description of it. For men – and it will usually be men – who like that kind of orthodoxy in their listening, it was the only decent record I ever made. For a few hardcore lo-fi fans, it remained the worst thing I'd yet made. For me, it's roughly like my own equivalent of the Beatles *Sgt Pepper* album. In terms of sound quality and careful musicianship it may well be my finest hour. But it's not necessarily my best album.

LESSON 25
THE PRODUCER KNOWS BEST... USUALLY

If you're going to work with a producer then it's a good idea, mostly, to do as you are asked to do. Because if you have made the decision to work him/her because you liked their ideas, then trust them. For the duration of this exercise, the producer should be the chief. Otherwise, don't do it.

When I worked with Andy Partridge he was highly regarded within the music industry, whereas I, even by those who'd heard of me, was considered to be an awkward and somewhat spiky character: a reasonable songwriter perhaps but a difficult prospect.

In the event, Andy and I worked very well together and I only held out for my own way on a couple of really minor things. On both occasions it wasn't because I couldn't do as I was being asked, but because stylistically I wouldn't normally have done such a thing. My reasoning was that I was making a Martin Newell album, not an XTC album. Andy graciously accepted this. My advice therefore, when you're working with a producer, is to do as you're asked. But to hold out if a thing really doesn't feel right for you.

Me and Andy Partridge at Porky's in Shaftesbury Avenue mastering the Greatest Living Englishman

ROCK STARS' OTHER TALENTS

In my spare time I collect stories about famous musicians' other jobs. Although some of these stories are well-known among music fans, I've found that the wider public is often unaware of them. When the American rock'n'roll legend Eddie Cochran died in a car crash just outside Chippenham in April 1960, the first officer at the scene was PC Dave Harman of the Wiltshire Constabulary. The young policeman changed his name to Dave Dee, later notching up a string of 1960s chart hits with his band. They were called Dave Dee, Dozy, Beaky, Mick & Tich.

In 1981, the Tamla Motown soul legend Marvin Gaye, mentally exhausted by fame and drug abuse, disappeared to Ostend, Belgium, a city of about 70,000 people. Here he led a reportedly abstemious life for over a year, staying anonymously at the family home of a Belgian music promoter. He went jogging on the beaches, he played darts with the locals, and sometimes, when they were busy, he helped out at his favourite café. Nearly nobody guessed his identity. One café customer even asked the proprietor, "Did you know that your waiter looks a lot like Marvin Gaye?" When the singer had recovered, he resumed his music career, returning to the charts in 1982 with the award-winning 'Sexual Healing'. Unfortunately, two years later, at home in the USA while involved in a family dispute, he was shot through the heart by his father and died.

Sterling Morrison, guitarist with the influential Velvet Underground, after leaving the band in the 1970s, qualified as a master mariner and spent much of the 1980s as the captain of a Houston tugboat. Over in the UK meanwhile, Rose Simpson who'd played in the Incredible String Band, darlings of the late 1960s hippy scene, became an academic, an author and, for a while, the Mayor of Aberystwyth.

While at least two members of post-punk band the Housemartins, went on to greater music-biz glory, their bespectacled guitarist, Stan Cullimore became a successful and prolific children's author. Buster Bloodvessel, of the 1980s ska band Bad Manners, opened a hotel in Margate for large people who liked their grub. It was called Fatty Towers. It lasted for two years until Buster, whose real name is Doug Trendle, had to give it up – for health reasons.

Over in the science department, Brian Cox, former keyboard player of chart-topping 90s stars D:Ream ('Things Can Only Get Better') became a professor of particle physics and a pin-up of popular science. Similarly, Sir Brian May was already mega-famous for some decades as Queen's guitarist before it emerged that he was also an astro-physicist, later to be appointed Chancellor of Liverpool John Moore's University. My closer research turned up far too many of Sir Brian May's other honours and accolades to list here.

Brian May, incidentally, teamed up with his friend, the much-missed Sir Patrick Moore to write a book *The Complete History of the Universe*. Sir Patrick hated pop music but was a keen pianist and an outstanding xylophone player. In earlier days he'd accompanied Einstein on piano while the latter played Saint-Saëns on his violin. You won't believe this either, but in 1981, Moore performed a solo xylophone rendition of the Sex Pistols 'Anarchy in the UK' at a Royal Variety Performance.

Music stars who bypass the excesses of fame sometimes prove highly successful in other fields. One of the best known of these is Jeff 'Skunk' Baxter, guitar wizard of Steely Dan, who astonishingly became a senior ballistic missiles defence advisor to the US Government. He was an early computer buff who went deeper into the rabbit hole. While reading an aviation magazine he realised that computer research, which he'd done for music technology, might also serve military purposes. He submitted a paper on the subject. The somewhat surprised top brass at the Pentagon eventually drafted him into service as a defence consultant, where he remains highly respected to this day.

Baxter also brought his lateral thinking to the defence table: "We thought turntables were for playing records until rappers began to use them as instruments. We thought airplanes were for carrying passengers until terrorists realised they could be used as missiles." he said. So there we have it, all you enemies of the Free West. You may have your super weapons. But in goal, we have Jeff 'Skunk' Baxter, who played on Steely Dan's *Countdown to Ecstasy*.

In popular music, we find that talent goes to talent in much the same way as money goes to money. Lady Gaga, for instance, won a BAFTA award as Best Actress in *A Star is Born*. Traffic frequently goes the other way, however. The late comedian Norman Wisdom – regarded as a comedy demi-god in Albania – taught himself to play the piano, trumpet, saxophone, flute, drums, bugle and clarinet. The late Roy Castle described as 'Dancer, singer, comedian, actor, TV presenter and musician', could play many different instruments. Note that 'musician' is listed last. The 19th-century essayist Walter Pater wrote that, "All art constantly aspires towards the condition of music." We really *do* love music. Sometimes, we just hold it cheap, that's all.

LESSON 26
REMEMBER YOU'VE GOT OTHER TALENTS TOO

During one of the many periods when I needed to leave the music business for a while in order to make some money for various luxuries, like food and footwear, I became a performance poet. This was at the beginning of the 1990s. Through a series of happy accidents, being in the right place at the right time – oh, and working very hard – I soon became unexpectedly successful. I was sometimes booked by schools to talk to the kids about poetry and lyrics. This is what I told them that I'd learned:

"You may have a dream, say, that you want to be a singer, or an actor, or an artist. You may soon discover that you have a talent for your chosen art form. You may even be very good at it. But just because you do seem to be good, or even outstanding at singing, acting or art, never assume that it is your only talent – or even your best talent. Do at least try other forms. When I was at school I was always good at writing and poetry. But I wanted to be a pop singer. When I got in a band, it was usually me who wrote the songs – and nearly always the words. Despite early hints that I might have had talent as a writer, it never occurred to me to do anything other than persist with my battered dreams of being a pop singer. Only when I had briefly given up on the idea and begun writing almost from despair, did I discover that I could make a living from it. So don't make my mistake. You will almost certainly have a second or third talent. It may even be your best or strongest talent. Go and search for it, then try to develop it."

SPACE

Leaving some space in a piece of music is one of the most important parts of the home recording jigsaw. Across all of the arts, in fact, whether it's writing, painting, drama, dance or music, the use of space – and its close companion silence – is a thing which most demonstrates an artist's experience and maturity within their chosen field. Space, as they used to proclaim at the beginning of *Star Trek* episodes, is 'the final frontier'.

The subject of leaving space is rarely taught, let alone encouraged, in the production of music. When we are learning about pop music, very few clues about the role of space are immediately apparent. Jazz musicians, for instance, often used to say to younger musicians, "It ain't the notes which you play – it's the ones you don't play." Cryptic as this expression sounded to me when I first ever heard it, I now understand exactly what these older players whom I spoke to were getting at. The temptation to use everything, when you have an armoury of musical instruments and effects at your disposal, can sometimes be overwhelming. As can the temptation, for a technically able or ego-driven guitarist, when asked to play a solo, to use every lick in their locker.

Many musical solos seem to me, anyway, to be so much willy waving. To over-complicate a piece of music with what the player regards as their own technical excellence is often, I think, usually a male trait, rather than a female one, It's also boring, boorish, and at times deeply annoying to encounter. Many people too, may mistake the ownership of equipment and their technical knowledge of it, with having a 'professional attitude'.

There were once publications aimed at such players. *International Musician and Recording World*, was one example. It ran between the mid-1970s and the early 1990s. As a magazine it was highly successful, well-distributed and read by many amateur and aspiring musicians. It featured interviews with professional recording engineers, bassists, drummers, keyboardists, guitarists and producers.

As a non-technical sort of person, I found most of its contents fairly dull. I can't remember ever getting through an entire article, let alone the mag itself. Again, the whole subject of technical equipment and any know-how around it seemed a particularly male province, one which I found myself instinctively rebelling against. I wanted to make pop music. I wanted to do it now. I wanted it to be fun. I wanted the music to sound cheap, slightly flawed and instant. Surely we didn't need all this gear, all this tech spec – all this waffle? Apart from anything else, in my mid-20s I had very little money and wasn't even a particularly good musician.

But I could write a song and I could string a reasonable lyric together. I knew some good chords and I was determined not to travel a conventional route within the music biz. I also knew how a band worked, because by 26 I'd been playing live in bands for six years. For five of those years, I'd also been teaching myself slowly about home-recording on my Sony reel-to-reel machine. Over hundreds of recordings, I'd gradually begun to learn that simplicity was just as valid as complexity in the creation of music.

Many musicians, some of them quite well-known and technically brilliant, still don't know about space. For me, giving things room to breathe has loomed large. Some people never discover space. Others get it straight away. It took me a little while. In fact, I'm still learning.

Certain old blues musicians understood space very well. Sadly, many of their English imitators never get it. Studio One dub reggae artists of the mid-1970s understood space, because it gave them a place to exercise their endlessly repeating echoes. The Essex R&B band Dr Feelgood used space so well that they almost single-handedly inspired the punk rock movement. And what was punk, after all, but the sound of three-minute pop music refreshing itself by clearing out all the slush? At the other side of the spectrum, Brian Wilson of the Beach Boys understood space as did the Beatles and their producer George Martin.

So what can we learn here? When you record a song, imagine that you begin with an empty room. Where do we start? Maybe put the carpets down first, with their underlay: the drums, a single piano or a guitar. Now invite a dancer in – the song itself. And how is the lighting? Still not quite right? Remove something. Take out the carpets, let the dancer work on the floorboards. Maybe by moonlight.

I've stretched this comparison but you'll get the picture. You now have a room with a dancer in it. Everything else is so much furniture and décor. When you're having trouble with a recording, don't add something new. First strip it back down to the rhythm track and the vocal. Then began to move things back into the room, one by one. It's sometimes said that hunger is the best condiment. Well, space can be the best backing band. Learn how to use it.

Go and listen to 'Fever' by Peggy Lee. It features a stand-up bass, some finger-clicks, a few tom-tom punctuation marks and Peggy Lee's voice. Massive international hit. Nearly nothing on it. It's timeless pop music by any standards. One of the things that has blighted pop music over the decades is professional musicians marching in, pushing everyone else out of the way and showing the little boys how they think it should be done.

The band Cream (1966-1969) were an example of this. They had their moments, of course. But they were a jazz combo in many respects, rather than a pop group. They held a farewell concert at the Royal Albert Hall in late 1968, the three of them all thundering away like a road-gang building a big ugly motorway, while an audience of hippy twats shook their heads in pseudo-religious fervour. It's very common to say that these virtuosi were wasted on pop music. The truth was that pop music was wasted on them.

There were two famous chart hits of that same era: 'Love Grows' by Edison Lighthouse (1970) and 'Everlasting Love' by Love Affair (1968). Both of these gems have never stopped sounding great and neither song has really dated. Conversely, the Albert Hall *Farewell Concert* by Cream is still talked about reverentially by a few old men who like to crap on about the virtues of that sort of musicianship. 'Love Grows' and 'Everlasting Love' will still get people singing along on building sites who weren't even alive when the records were made. Why is this? Well, my own theory is that the makers of those two pop records knew about the importance of space. So did the members of Cream. But *they* looked down upon pop music and even if they did recognise the importance of space, they certainly didn't apply it to their farewell concert.

Since the days of Phil Spector's 'Wall of Sound' in the early 1960s, there's been a natural tendency in certain quarters to think that bigger is better and more is more. Space was something that Phil Spector almost certainly knew about, but mostly chose not to employ. His contemporary George 'Shadow' Morton, on the other hand, whose best work was probably with the Shangri-Las, made records just as 'big' as Spector's but knew a little more about the concept of using space.

What I've learned after all these years is this: when you are making a recording and it's sounding pretty good – even though you don't feel it's quite finished – take a mix of it and sleep on it. Or you may have been slaving for hours on a recording and then your partner, or your mum, passes through the room, saying, "Aw... I think I preferred it when it just had the guitar and your voice." Well, before you put all that other stuff on it, do at least *consider* their opinion. Leaving space in your creations is not quite the same as 'less is more' or 'show don't tell' – but it's working in a similar area. So, if the recording's not quite right, before you add something new, think about removing something, before you start again.

That's all. Dismissed.

OTHER TITLES FROM DUNLIN PRESS INCLUDE

PORT
An anthology of writing from across the UK and beyond, via giant container docks and small fishing villages, with a breadth of style as diverse as the ports and harbours themselves.

Boot Sale Harvest, by Adrian May
Author, poet and songwriter Adrian May takes a seasonal journey through the car-boot fields of Essex that artist Grayson Perry has described as being like a "casual museum".

Objects
A collection of contemporary poetry and experimental writing from 25 authors including Emma Bolland, Martyn Crucefix, Kitty Doherty, Joshua Martin, Vik Shirley and Richard Skinner.

Pomes Flixus, by MW Bewick
Poems that are a collision of constantly shifting perspectives – a series of sometimes startling evocations of life in the modern world, sharp with considerations of culture, class and the use of language itself.

Find out more at dunlinpress.com

www.ingramcontent.com/pod-product-compliance
Lightning Source LLC
Chambersburg PA
CBHW030552080526
44585CB00012B/354